T0248276

WALKING IN AROLLA AND ZINAL

THE VAL D'HÉRENS AND VAL D'ANNIVIERS IN THE SWISS VALAIS

by Jonathan and Lesley Williams

JUNIPER HOUSE, MURLEY MOSS,
OXENHOLME ROAD, KENDAL, CUMBRIA LA9 7RL
www.cicerone.co.uk

© Jonathan and Lesley Williams 2024
First edition 2024
ISBN: 9781786310965

Printed by Bell & Bain, Glasgow, on responsibly sourced paper
and other controlled sources.
A catalogue record for this book is available from the British Library.
All photographs are by the authors unless otherwise stated.

Route mapping by Lovell Johns www.lovelljohns.com

Updates to this guide

While every effort is made by our authors to ensure the accuracy of guide-books as they go to print, changes can occur during the lifetime of an edition. Any updates that we know of for this guide will be on the Cicerone website (www.cicerone.co.uk/1096/updates), so please check before planning your trip. We also advise that you check information about such things as transport, accommodation and shops locally. Even rights of way can be altered over time. We are always grateful for information about any discrepancies between a guidebook and the facts on the ground, sent by email to updates@cicerone.co.uk or by post to Cicerone, Juniper House, Murley Moss, Oxenholme Road, Kendal, LA9 7RL.

Register your book: To sign up to receive free updates, special offers and GPX files where available, register your book in your Cicerone library at www.cicerone.co.uk.

Note on mapping

The route maps in this guide are derived from publicly available data, data-bases and crowd-sourced data. As such they have not been through the detailed checking procedures that would generally be applied to a published map from an official mapping agency. However, we have reviewed them closely in light of local knowledge as part of the preparation of this guide.

Front cover: Lac d'Arpitettaz and the mountain wall between the Weisshorn and Zinalrothorn (Walk 31)

CONTENTS

Lac d'Arpitettaz and the mountain wall between the Weisshorn and Zinalrothorn (Walk 31)

Symbols used on route maps

route		P	parking
alternative route		◉	bus stop
start point/alt start point		🍴	restaurant
finish point		⊕	groceries/shop
start/finish point		⬠	hotel
route direction			
glacier			
woodland			
urban areas			
regional border			
international border			
station/railway			
peak			
manned/unmanned refuge			
campsite			
building			
church/cross			
pass			
viewpoint			
bridge			
other feature			
cable car			
water feature			

Relief
in metres

4000–4200	
3800–4000	
3600–3800	
3400–3600	
3200–3400	
3000–3200	
2800–3000	
2600–2800	
2400–2600	
2200–2400	
2000–2200	
1800–2000	
1600–1800	
1400–1600	
1200–1400	
1000–1200	
800–1000	
600–800	
400–600	
200–400	
0–200	

SCALE: 1:50,000

0 kilometres 0.5   1

0 miles   0.5

Contour lines are drawn at 25m intervals and highlighted at 100m intervals.

GPX files for all routes can be downloaded free at www.cicerone.co.uk/1096/GPX.

Mountain safety

Every mountain walk has its dangers, and those described in this guidebook are no exception. All who walk or climb in the mountains should recognise this and take responsibility for themselves and their companions along the way. The author and publisher have made every effort to ensure that the information contained in this guide was correct when it went to press, but, except for any liability that cannot be excluded by law, they cannot accept responsibility for any loss, injury or inconvenience sustained by any person using this book.

International distress signal *(emergency only)*
Six blasts on a whistle (and flashes with a torch after dark) spaced evenly for one minute, followed by a minute's pause. Repeat until an answer is received. The response is three signals per minute followed by a minute's pause.

Helicopter rescue
The following signals are used to communicate with a helicopter:

Help needed:
raise both arms
above head to
form a 'Y'

Help not needed:
raise one arm
above head, extend
other arm downward

Emergency telephone numbers
If telephoning from the UK the dialling codes are:
Switzerland: 0041; *USA:* 011 41

Switzerland: OCVS (Organisation Cantonale Valaisanne de Secours): tel 144

Weather reports
Switzerland: tel 162 (in French, German or Italian), www.meteoschweiz.ch/en

Mountain rescue can be very expensive – be adequately insured.

ROUTE SUMMARY TABLE

Walk	Route	Start/finish
Val d'Hérens and Val d'Hérémence		
Val d'Hérémence (Dix)		
1	Thyon to Grande Dixence barrage	Thyon/Hotel du Barrage
2	Grande Dixence barrage to Cabane des Dix	Hotel du Barrage/Cabane des Dix
3	Cabane des Dix to Arolla	Cabane des Dix/Arolla
Arolla		
4	Pas de Chèvres from Arolla	Arolla
5	Cabane des Aiguilles Rouges from Arolla	Arolla poste
6	Lac Bleu circular walk from Arolla	Arolla village centre
7	Plan Bertol from Arolla	Arolla
8	Cabane de la Tsa from Arolla	Arolla poste
9	Arolla to Les Haudères – the valley route	Arolla poste/Les Haudères bus stop
10	Arolla to Evolène – the high Route 6	Arolla poste/Evolène
Les Haudères and Ferpècle		
11	Roc Vieux from Les Haudères	Les Haudères
12	Ferpècle valley	Les Haudères village centre bus stop
13	Bricola and the upper Ferpècle valley	Ferpècle bus stop at Les Salays
Evolène		
14	Tour of the rock villages – Route 214	Evolène village centre
15	Evolène to Pralong (Dix valley) via Col de la Meina	Evolène/Pralong
16	Pic d'Artsinol	La Meina/Chemeuille at the top of the Lanna ski lift
17	Evolène to Pralong (Dix valley) via Mandelon	Top of chairlift from Lanna/Pralong
18	Euseigne pyramids, Ossona, the passerelle and Combioule hot springs	Euseigne village bus stop
19	Villa to Grimentz via Col de Torrent	Villa/Grimentz
20	La Sage to Cabane de Moiry via Col du Tsaté	La Sage/Cabane de Moiry
21	Evolène to Cabane des Becs de Bosson	Evolène/Cabane des Becs de Bosson

Distance	Time	Ascent	Descent	Grade	Page
17.5km	6hr	780m	740m	2	40
12.5km	5hr	900m	110m	2–3	45
12.5km	4hr 30min	460m	1380m	3	50
11.5km	4hr 30min	860m	860m	2	55
13.5km	5hr 45min	1100m	1100m	3	58
9.5km	3hr 45min	540m	540m	2	62
12km	4hr 30min	750m	750m	3	66
9.5km	4hr	860m	860m	2	70
9.5km	2hr 15min	100m	660m	1–2	74
15km	5hr 30min	860m	1500m	3	78
12km	5hr	950m	950m	2	82
16km	5hr	660m	660m	2	86
11km	4hr 20min	660m	660m	2	90
12km	4hr	570m	570m	1–2	93
15.5km	6hr 30min	1410m	1180m	3	98
11km	4hr 30min	900m	900m	2–3	102
12km	3hr 40min	250m	760m	2	106
12km	4hr	610m	610m	2	110
17km	6hr 15min	1200m	1350m	2–3	114
11.5km	6hr	1700m	550m	3	119
11.5km	5hr	1710m	100m	2–3	124

Walk	Route	Start/finish
Val d'Anniviers and Val de Moiry		
Réchy valley		
22	Cabane des Becs de Bosson to Nax	Cabane des Becs de Bosson/Nax
23	Réchy valley	Le Crêt du Midi
Moiry valley		
24	Grimentz to Cabane des Becs de Bosson	Grimentz/Cabane des Becs de Bosson
25	Cabane des Becs de Bosson to Cabane de Moiry	Cabane des Becs de Bosson/Cabane de Moiry
26	Lac Moiry circuit 2500m	Moiry Barrage
27	Cabane de Moiry to Zinal	Cabane de Moiry/Zinal
Zinal		
28	Zinal to Cabane du Petit Mountet	Zinal
29	Zinal to Cabane du Grand Mountet	Zinal/Cabane du Grand Mountet
30	Roc de la Vache from Zinal	Zinal
31	Cabane Arpitettaz from Zinal	Zinal/Cabane Arpitettaz
32	Cabane de Tracuit from Zinal	Zinal/Cabane de Tracuit
Hotel Weisshorn and Chandolin		
33	Chandolin, Planets Trail, Hotel Weisshorn to Zinal	Chandolin/Zinal
34	Bella Tola from Tignousa	Tignousa
35	Illhorn, Illsee, Lac Noir and Cabane Bella-Tola;	Le Tsapé/Tignousa
Multi-day routes		
	Tour du Val d'Hérens (TVH)	Thyon/Nax
	Tour des Cabanes du Val d'Anniviers (TCVA)	Grimentz/Zinal

Distance	Time	Ascent	Descent	Grade	Page
13.7km	4hr 30min	100m	1820m	2–3	137
15km	5hr	650m	650m	2	141
9km	4hr 30min	1430m	40m	2	145
16.7km	5hr 30min	850m	1000m	3	148
14.2km	5hr	630m	630m	2	152
16km	6hr 30min	720m	1870m	2–3	156
13km	4hr 30min	620m	620m	1–2	159
11km (22km round trip)	5hr (9–10hr round trip)	1290m (1370m round trip)	80m (1370m round trip)	3–4	162
15km	5hr 30min	940m	940m	2	166
11km (22km round trip)	4hr 30min (3hr 30min return, 8hr round trip)	1155m (1200m round trip)	45m (1200m round trip)	3	170
9km (18km round trip)	4hr 45min (3hr 15min return, 8hr round trip)	1600m (1620m round trip)	20m (1620m round trip)	3	173
20km	6hr 15min	650m	950m	2	177
11.5km	4hr 30min	880m	880m	3	182
10km	4hr	520m	820m	2	185
77.7km	27hr (5 days)	4210m	5050m	3	128
87km	36hr (6–7 days)	6730m	6650m	3–4	189

Looking south towards the Weisshorn from the Bella Tola ridge (Walk 34)

INTRODUCTION

Looking down onto the village of Zinal

THE VALAIS – VAL D'ANNIVIERS AND VAL D'HÉRENS

It was a hot afternoon and my feet were beginning to feel a bit weary as I walked back down the beautiful Ferpècle valley after a long day exploring the glaciers and enjoying the views of the Dent Blanche in the valley's upper reaches. Hearing a car approaching from behind, I stuck out my thumb and the car pulled over. The tiny interior was crammed with four ladies and festooned with streamers and balloons – they had been to a wedding and the associated festivities – but they happily squashed up and gave me a lift. Chatting in my rusty French, I explained I first visited the valley in 1976 and have returned whenever possible over the years. The driver explained that she loved the valley so much that she returned every year for the entire summer. Such is the magic of the Val d'Hérens and its friendly people.

Within the canton of Valais, and a little to the west of world-famous Zermatt, two French-speaking valleys run parallel to their more glamourous neighbour, a world apart yet matching or surpassing it in their beauty and potential as an ideal alpine walking destination. Val d'Anniviers is known to skiers, the lift systems of Grimentz, Chandolin and Zinal providing rapid access to higher alpine paths, while the Val d'Hérens' principal village of Evolène remains attractive and traditional, as does the whole of the valley and the higher alpine centre of Arolla. Both valleys are surrounded by impressive peaks

From Pic d'Artsinol, the view extends from the Weisshorn (left) to Mont Blanc (far right) (Walk

and glaciers, including the Dent Blanche, are easily accessible from the Rhône valley, with a regular and comprehensive bus service, and have a good range of facilities. They are explored by trekkers walking from Chamonix to Zermatt, many returning time and time again to enjoy further exploration in this unique and friendly region.

The canton of Valais covers a large area in south-west Switzerland between the Italian border and the Rhône valley. The Val d'Anniviers and Val d'Hérens explored in this guide run south from the vineyards and wine-production centres in the French-speaking (*romande*) part of the Rhône valley. The highest mountains of the Valais are in the eastern, German-speaking area around Zermatt, the grandeur of the Matterhorn and Monte Rosa providing challenges for mountaineers and a superb environment for walkers to explore the vast network of paths covered in the Cicerone guide *Walking in Zermatt and Saas-Fee*.

The settlement of these valleys is some of the earliest in the Alps, and many of the early timber-framed houses and barns are lovingly maintained. Farming continues in the villages and surrounding meadows and pastures today, often in much the same way as in times gone by. In summer, sheep, goats and cattle graze the high meadows of the Alps, and in winter the animals live in farm buildings or are taken to the lower valleys. Festivals that celebrate the beginning and end of summer, when animals are moved to and from high pastures, include cow-fighting contests in both spring and autumn, and other seasonal celebrations. You may hear locals speaking in a valley patois when chatting together, but English is generally understood and spoken.

Many of the walks described in this guide are long and high but on well-maintained paths; they are not usually hard, although some high passes require care, especially in snow. Trips to high huts in the shadows of the peaks are a big element of the walking, while lower down in the valleys, from the ski resorts of Zinal, Grimentz, Chandolin and St Luc, and from Evolène in the Val d'Hérens, lifts carry walkers to higher routes and walkers' peaks with vistas from the Bernese mountains in the north to the assembly of 4000m peaks along the southern border with Italy.

Geology

The Alps are relatively young mountains in geological time, having formed between 40 and 25 million years ago when the African plate and Eurasian plate collided, pressing and folding the continental crust and forcing both plates upwards. This caused the Eurasian plate to become squashed and stretched beneath, resulting in a layer of gneiss from the ancient African continental plate sitting on top of younger rocks that originated in ancient oceans. The huge Rhône valley to the north was caused by a fault line, and the glaciers and river that carved their way through followed this natural line of weakness.

The Val d'Hérens and Val d'Anniviers were formed during successive ice ages, with many huge glaciers carving out the main valleys and higher hanging valleys, all eventually feeding into the Rhône valley. There have been many glaciation periods, particularly during the last 2 million years, and the last one, known as the Würm glaciation, took place between 80,000 and 10,000 years ago. More recently the Little Ice Age between the 14th and 19th centuries saw advances in the glaciers, their retreat leaving huge lateral moraines, which are particularly noticeable beside the Tsijiore Nouve glacier above Arolla and other higher regions of the Arolla, Dix, Ferpècle, Moiry and the Val d'Anniviers valleys. Many paths in the area traverse or run along the crest of these moraines.

The current accelerated retreat of the glaciers has seen over 100 glaciers disappear in Switzerland alone and those of this region halve in volume. In the geology and glaciology museum in Les Haudères you will discover how the glaciers stretched far down into the valleys, with helpful exhibits providing more information about the formation of the mountains. How things have changed in recent times; the bare, scoured rock immediately below the snouts of all the glaciers bears testament to the rapid retreat of the ice, while algae growing on many glaciers turns them pink – another sign of dying glaciers.

Plants and wildlife

For much of the year the alpine slopes in both valleys are covered with snow. The blanket of snow acts as protection for hardy little plants while they rest in a semi-hibernating state. As the

*Spring gentian (*Gentiana verna*); edelweiss (*Leontopodium alpinum*); bladder campion (*Silene vulgaris*)

snow begins to melt, myriad varieties of alpine flowers bloom in succession in the short summer season. The first to appear is the alpine snowbell (*Soldanella*), tiny fringed pink/purple flowers supported on thin stems. In June more plants come into flower, mainly pink or purple in colour, including the Carthusian pink (a relative of the garden pink), cowberry and varieties of campion, stonecrop, saxifrage, orchid and cinquefoil. In July the alpenrose transforms many of the hillsides in the area into a sea of vivid

rose red. This slow-growing plant can colonise huge areas of both open hillside and lightly shaded woodland. Other flowers to look out for are the intensely blue gentian and, as autumn approaches, the delicate meadow saffron or autumn crocus. To identify these, and many others you will come across, help is at hand. With photographs of flowers arranged by colour, *Alpine Flowers* by Gillian Price, published by Cicerone, provides an easy way to identify 230 alpine flowers.

The Val d'Anniviers and Val d'Hérens both provide quieter high mountain locations for ibex and chamois, and there is a very good chance that you will spot these wonderful creatures when walking the higher, less visited routes. Ibex, in particular, are known to live and graze near the Prafleuri refuge to the west of the Dixence *barrage* (dam) and in the upper reaches of the valley leading from Arolla to the Pas de Chèvres. Chamois have short, slender horns and tend to live and feed in small family groups, while ibex have longer, thicker, ridged horns.

Take a walk across any high alpine meadow and you may hear a piercing whistle repeated over and over again. The sound comes from a marmot, a small brown rodent about the size of a mountain hare. As it stands upright sounding the alarm, others may be seen scampering across the grass, heading for their burrows, where they hibernate during the winter months. Meanwhile on the lower slopes and in woodland tiny red black squirrels scuttle around at great speed, foraging for berries and vegetation.

The skies are the preserve of the Alpine chough, a close relative of the crow, and eagles can often be spotted riding the thermals high above the hillsides.

Climbing

The valleys have been a centre of alpine climbing for over 150 years. The Weisshorn (4505m), bordering the Val d'Anniviers and Mattertal, was first climbed in 1861. The Dent Blanche (4357m), standing just to the north of the line of peaks that form the border with Italy, is a similarly

Roc Vieux with the Dents de Veisivi from Lac Bleu (Walk 6)

The Moiry icefall seen from Cabane de Moiry (Walk 25)

serious undertaking for mountaineers and was first climbed in 1862. The Zinalrothorn (4221m) was first climbed in 1864, and the following year first ascents of the Ober Gabelhorn (4063m) and Mont Blanc de Cheilon (3870m) were achieved, the same year as the first ascent of the Matterhorn (4478m). Difficult lower peaks such as Mont Collon (3637m) had to wait until 1867 for a first ascent.

With its four 4000m peaks, Zinal is an alpine centre, while the lower and generally easier peaks around the Val d'Hérens have attracted both experienced and novice alpinists for many decades.

THE WALKING

The walks included in this guide range from straightforward strolls to mountain villages and restaurants, lakes and viewpoints, which may take a couple of hours with modest up and down, through to serious mountain challenges: full-day walks with some exposure and cable support and routes to high refuges used by mountaineers. Between these, and comprising most of the guide, are mountain paths with short and long walks to mountain huts and passes and a few walking peaks.

Most walks are on well-maintained mountain paths with occasional short, more exciting sections, all marked with traditional red-and-white signage. Some more challenging routes follow steep, rocky high alpine trails with handholds, ladders or metal steps and long drops. So, the walking is varied: short, straightforward routes in the valleys lead to restaurants, lakes and waterfalls; middle-mountain walks take in high restaurants and cols with superb, heart-stopping views; and higher routes climb to walking peaks and huts. There is choice for everyone here.

A note about patous, the dogs guarding sheep. These dogs live with the flock and are there to protect them. If they approach you, stop and remain quiet and motionless. Keep walking poles close to your body so you don't appear threatening. The dog will take a few moments to look at you and decide that you are of no threat. They may bark, which can be intimidating. You will be safe to continue when the dog moves off, but move slowly at first and keep quiet as you pass. Make a circuit round the flock if you see one ahead.

Walks in the lower valley

Mainly outside the scope of this guide, the lower parts of the valleys also have fine walks, often with exceptional views looking out over the Rhône and the mountains to the north. In the Val d'Hérens such walks include the Bisses trail, Swiss Route 58, which starts at Grimentz and finishes close to Martigny. It's a good walk but not as flat as might be expected from a *bisse* (water channel) path, and there are

limited sections of actual bisse. Route 215, running from near Vernamiège to La Luette, takes in sections of restored mountain landscape, the agritourism hamlet of Ossona and the 133m Grande Combe *passerelle* (suspension bridge). The best bits of this are covered in Walk 18, which also takes in the hot springs of Combioule and the Euseigne pyramids.

Many paths provide good walks around the villages of Hérémence and Les Collons and up to the resort of Thyon, but these tend to be more affected by ski infrastructure and are out of character with the mountain walking towards the heads of the valleys. Likewise, there are opportunities near St Martin, but these can be difficult to access by public transport and often mean a trip to Sion to reach start or finish points. Car-parking opportunities are not abundant!

In the Val d'Anniviers there are fewer good walking opportunities around the valley entrances. We have included walks in the unique Val de Réchy and around Grimentz, across the valley from Chandolin and Tignousa, but not the lower-level wooded paths around Vissoie and Mission.

Local tourist offices have brochures on walks that tend to be easier than the mountain walks providing the main focus of this guide. These include the Marmot Trail above Arolla, several 'Route des Eaux' walks around Arolla and the Dix valley and the 'Routes des Roches' around La

Sage, La Forclaz and Villa. With many hundreds of kilometres of paths in both main valleys, there is plenty of scope for exploring and finding new trails.

High cols

The walking and treks in this area require the crossing of some high cols. Those between the Val d'Hérens and Val de Moiry – the Pas de Lona, the Col de Torrent and the Col du Tsaté – are high but straightforward. Likewise, the cols between Zinal and Gruben are unproblematic under summer conditions. The approaches to the high huts of Grand Mountet, Arpitetta and Tracuit are trickier and involve some aided sections.

The crossings between the Val des Dix and the Val d'Hérens may also present challenges. The Pas de Chèvres is crossed by a series of ladders after an approach over crumbly glacial moraine, while the Col de Riedmatten is a stern pull up an eroded shale gully. Both sound and look worse than they are, but you should be prepared, especially if conditions are poor. At the time of writing, the Pas de Chèvres is not recommended as the route to the ladders has become difficult, although we understand there are plans for major improvements – check locally before attempting.

Trekking routes

This area is also visited by some of Europe's best trekking routes.

Chamonix–Zermatt Walker's Haute Route Winding over passes between Chamonix and Zermatt, the Walkers' Haute Route takes nearly two weeks to complete, crossing the canton of Valais in the southern part of Switzerland. It enters the area covered by this book near the Prafleuri refuge and continues to Arolla, Les Haudères and Zinal before heading to the remote Gruben valley and the Augstbordpass above St Niklaus, and onwards to Zermatt.

Alpine Passes Route (Swiss National Route 6) This 695km ultra long-distance trail runs from Chur in eastern Switzerland to the shores of Lac Léman. Usually described east to west, it enters the Val d'Anniviers over the Meidpass, descending to Ayer just north of Zinal, across to Grimentz, then to Evolène via the Cabane des Becs de Bosson. The route then heads to Arolla, over to Cabane des Dix, then north to Cabane de Prafleuri, where it leaves the scope of this guidebook and heads to Cabane de Louvie, Mauvoisin and onwards. Several routes in this guide use sections of Route 6.

Tour du Val d'Hérens (TVH) This five- to six-day tour begins by following a superb balcony route above the Hérémence valley between Thyon and the Dixence barrage. The route continues to Cabane des Dix, over the Col de Riedmatten to Arolla and down the valley to Les Haudères. Climbing above the Val d'Hérens towards Becs des Bosson, the trail traverses remote regions before descending to Nax overlooking the Rhône valley at the end of the tour.

Tour des Cabanes du Val d'Anniviers (TCVA) This tour links a range of high mountain refuges above Zinal. From Grimentz, the tour visits the Cabane des Becs de Bosson, Cabane de Moiry, Cabane du Petit Mountet, Cabane du Grand Mountet, Cabane Arpitettaz and Cabane de Tracuit before dropping to Zinal.

Sierre to Zinal Also called the 'Race of the Five 4000m Peaks', Sierre–Zinal is a scenic 31km international mountain marathon route that involves a 2200m elevation gain, a superb balcony route passing Hotel Weisshorn above the Val d'Anniviers, then a 1100m drop to Zinal. If walking the route (much of which is covered in Walk 33), you will doubtless

be passed by runners enjoying the challenge, but avoid race day – usually the second weekend in August.

BASES IN THE VAL D'HÉRENS

Evolène

The village of Evolène is the principal settlement in the more extensive municipality of the same name, which also includes Les Haudères, La Sage, Villa, La Forclaz, Ferpècle and Arolla. It's a fine, thriving village almost entirely made up of old houses and barns of decorated stone and old timber, with several hotels, apartments, a camp site, a tourist office, a good range of shops and businesses and a supermarket. Regular buses serving the valley provide all the public transport required. In addition to the

The Tour du Val d'Hérens is clearly signposted (Walk 1)

fantastic walking options, the village also offers tennis, trout fishing, a fitness circuit and a via ferrata, as well as climbing and paragliding. Largely unaffected by the trappings of a ski resort, it has one chairlift which runs throughout most of the summer season from Lanna, about 1.5km northwest of Evolène, up to La Meina (Chemeuille) at 2122m, providing easy access to paths leading to Pic d'Artsinol and Pointe de Mandelon.

Les Haudères

Sleepy Les Haudères is almost entirely composed of ancient wooden houses and barns, with a small chapel, a geology museum, three or four hotels and restaurants, a campsite and a handful of shops. It sits at a strategically important point below the Dents de Veisivi, with one road and valley leading up to La Forclaz, La Sage, Villa and the Ferpècle valley, while another road leads south up to Arolla. It serves as a transport hub, where buses arrive at a similar time in a small square, connecting to all points throughout the area.

Arolla

Although small, Arolla stands at a height of just over 2000m and has special importance as a hiking and climbing centre, as well as an essential stop for trekkers on the Tour du Val d'Hérens, Swiss Route 6, and the Chamonix–Zermatt Walker's Haute Route. With just a few hotels, a campsite, a small general store and an excellent sports shop, the village itself is centred around the square, where the valley buses terminate. More accommodation can be found

Ancient wooden barns and houses in Evolène

Artworks in the Val d'Hérens

above the village in another hotel and several apartment blocks. Walks from Arolla can be both easy and challenging and all grades between, exploring the breathtaking mountain and glacier scenery and routes over to the Cabane des Dix.

Hérémence

Villages in the Val d'Hérémence can also provide a good base for a walking holiday, as Vex and Hérémence have accommodation options and good transport. However, they are not well positioned for most of the walking routes described in this book. Purpose-built or massively extended ski villages such as Thyon and Les Collons should be avoided.

Vissoie

Located just north of where the two valleys branch, to either Zinal or Moiry, Vissoie is more of a small transport hub rather than a tourist destination, although there are two hotels, a few shops and a campsite in the village. Buses converge from all the surrounding villages, leading to 10min of intense activity in the village square, before departing in different directions.

Chandolin

Chandolin is one of Europe's highest permanently inhabited villages and more of a skiers' destination,

An elegant bridge spans the Navisence torrent, the Weisshorn directly ahead (Walk 31)

with several hotels and apartments perched in a series of terraces, its tourist information office and shops situated at about 2000m. Buzzing with activity during the winter, the village is quiet during the summer months when a chairlift rises to Le Tsapé from a roadside lift station 1km south-east of the village, giving access to a large network of paths leading to viewpoints, including the Illhorn (2717m), Illsee, Schwarzhorn (2790m) and a route to access Bella Tola (3025m), all walkers' peaks. Other activities based around Chandolin include mountain biking, scooters, archery and fishing.

St Luc
St Luc is a picturesque village on a sunny terrace on the road between Vissoie and Chandolin. It offers several hotels, apartments, restaurants and a small selection of shops, as well as a bike park, tennis and climbing facilities, all serving to make this a modest tourist centre. A funicular rises to Tignousa at 2184m, a few minutes' walk from the François-Xavier Bagnoud Observatory, and the start of several good walking routes leading to Bella Tola and several high passes. The popular Planet Walk (included in Walk 33), with information boards and installations representing the planets and other astronomical features, begins below the observatory and contours around the hillside before rising to the Hotel Weisshorn, above which is the final installation, representing Pluto.

Grimentz
The heart of the village is a charming collection of ancient houses and

barns with their focal point being the ancient Burgher House dating from 1550, all providing a picturesque core to the sprawling buildings that clamber up the steep hillside. There are three or four hotels, apartments and a number of restaurants, as well as a good variety of shops, sports shops and a supermarket. In summer a *télécabine* (gondola) provides a good service to Bendolla, offering easier access to the Becs de Bosson and Roc d'Orzival range, while a cable car to Sorebois provides access to Zinal and Moiry.

Zinal

At 1674m, Zinal lies at the far southern end of the valley road. The centre has an array of shops, tourist information and a small supermarket, while the older houses of the original village can be found just one street back. Unless you venture further, you would be unaware of large apartment developments to the east and south of the village as they are well hidden from the main street. It's a friendly resort in summer, with several small hotels and some good restaurants that also cater to the continuous stream of trekkers who pass through on the Chamonix–Zermatt Walker's Haute Route. To the south of Zinal, the valley extends over a largely flat area to sports facilities, a campsite and a couple of restaurants before various paths climb to the Cabane du Petit Mountet and other higher cabanes (refuges) mainly used by mountaineers to access the higher peaks that crown the head of the valley.

WHEN TO GO

The main walking season runs from mid June until mid September. September and October can be attractive months to visit, with good daytime temperatures cooling progressively at night and glorious autumn colours, although mountain huts, accommodation and restaurants will close over the period.

In southern Switzerland, close to the Italian border, the valleys have a generally warm and dry summer climate. However, high in the mountains local factors may have a greater impact on the weather. Hot air rising from lower valleys can bring storms, and the normal alpine thunderstorms of late afternoon will occur throughout the summer, particularly on humid days, so, ideally, start and finish each day in good time; a thunderstorm can make you wet and cold very quickly. If a low-pressure zone settles over southern Switzerland, it could be dreary for a day or two. Heatwaves affecting the rest of Europe also affect the valleys, but the altitude and the dryness of the mountain air make them more manageable.

In June and well into July, there may be late-lying snow above 2000m. Check conditions before arriving – there are a few webcams, so it is possible to inspect the mountainsides remotely. Tourist offices will have a clear, if perhaps cautious, view on which routes are open. In the summer, late-lying snow will be soft and frustrating. In more exposed places, however, often on north-facing slopes and other sheltered places where there is less direct sunshine, it is possible to come across névé (hard snow) or even ice, so look out for this. Unless you are equipped with an axe, crampons and poles, take another route.

Weather

Temperature and rainfall statistics for nearby Zermatt over the summer months are shown in the table. (There is no direct data for the higher villages in these valleys.)

GETTING THERE

Switzerland is very accessible and has an excellent public transport infrastructure. These valleys are, however, some distance from the main airports or access points into the country, so it is likely that it will take at least 2–3hr to reach either valley after first entering Switzerland.

By train

From the UK and Northern Europe the trip by rail will cost a little more and take a bit longer than flying, but it is perfectly feasible as well as more environmentally friendly. From the UK take the Eurostar to Paris then the TGV from the Gare de Lyon to Geneva or Lausanne, connecting with Sion or Sierre. (Other routes avoiding Paris are available.) London to Sion or Sierre can be booked on a single ticket through French railways (SNCF). It

	May	June	July	August	September	October
Average high (°C)	20	23	25	24	20	14
Average low (°C)	7	10	11	11	7	2
Average monthly total hours of sunshine	155	175	200	180	170	140
Average monthly rainfall (mm)	39	47	49	63	45	46

Source: weatherandclimate.com Sion weather-station data

may be worth splitting the booking at Geneva to take advantage of discount deals/cards on both the French and Swiss railways.

Rail journeys from Belgium and the Netherlands and other points in Northern Europe are also options and often shorter.

By road

Road access is through the French motorway system to Geneva or Basel, or further east through Germany. You will need a Swiss motorway *vignette* (sticker), which currently costs CHF55. If coming via Basel, the most direct route is via the Lötschberg Tunnel: a long railway tunnel under the Bernese Oberland from Kandersteg through which accompanied vehicles can be transported on trains. From Geneva, the motorway route is Lausanne–Martigny–Sion–Sierre; Sion is the access point to the Val d'Hérens, and Sierre for Val d'Anniviers.

By air

Switzerland's main airports are Geneva, Zurich and Basel. From each of these it is possible to take trains right through to Sion or Sierre and continue by bus. All three are served by both low-cost and full-service airlines within Europe, from the UK and internationally.

Discount cards

If you are planning to spend some time travelling within Switzerland, the main card to consider is the Half Fare Card, currently CHF120 for one month. This provides half-price travel throughout the country, including buses, trains and cable cars, so it is a good deal. The saving on the return journey from Geneva or Zurich to any of the resorts in the two valleys almost covers the cost of the card, so all additional travel thereafter benefits. An alternative option is the Swiss Travel Pass, available for shorter periods, providing unlimited use of bus, train and lake-ferry routes.

TRAVEL IN THE REGION

There are no trains in either of the valleys, so public transport is by bus. In each case regular services operate at least hourly, and often more frequently, from Sion and Sierre up the valleys. Frequent services also operate between the various villages and walking locations. Buses are PostBuses, providing a comprehensive transport service in the valleys, running from early morning to late evening. Services are punctual and reliable, and delays are rare.

In both valleys a passport, or Citizens' Pass, issued free by all accommodation providers, gives free access to buses in and around the villages above La Luette and Vissoie; however, the various lifts in the Val d'Anniviers are not covered by this scheme.

Approaching a suspension bridge on the Grand Mountet route (Walk 29)

Lifts

Cable cars, funiculars, gondolas and chairlifts are an integral part of the Alpine walking experience. There is just one chairlift in the Val d'Hérens, operating between Evolène (Lanna) and Chemeuille, for easier access to the walking routes to Pic d'Artsinol and around Pointe de Mandelon. The Val d'Anniviers is well supplied with gondolas and lifts, notably between Zinal and Grimentz, but the wild upper valley has no lifts so is the preserve of mountain walkers.

Accommodation

A wide range of good accommodation is available throughout the valleys. There are outstanding tourist offices in the main villages, which can assist with bookings, as well as helpful websites (see Appendix A).

Camping

There are five campsites in the Val d'Anniviers – at Vissoie, Mission, Zinal and two in Grimentz, while in the Val d'Hérens, campsites can be found in Evolène, Les Haudères and Arolla, and lower in the valley at Vex (see Appendix A). Prices vary but are generally between CHF10 and CHF12 plus a tourist tax of CHF3 per person per night, and between CHF6 and CHF10 for tents. With plentiful local restaurants and well-stocked village stores, this is a good, low-cost option.

Apartments

Many apartments are available to rent in the summer. Prices may be around CHF600–800 per week for very good 2-bedroom, 4-person apartments.

Hotels

Hotels are mostly of a moderate price range, although there are a few more luxurious options in the main ski

Lunchtime at the Sorebois gondola station (Walk 27)

resorts in the Val d'Anniviers, details of which are available through the tourist offices or directly online.

Huts and mountain inns

You may want to use mountain huts and other mountain accommodation as a base for a few days. Mountain huts are either operated by the Swiss Alpine Club (SAC) or are privately owned. Mountain inns are privately run, often offering more private accommodation as well as dormitories. Overnight stays will usually cost in the range of CHF60–80 per person, including dinner and breakfast. All will provide a picnic lunch, if requested in good time, at an additional cost. Contact information for these huts is in Appendix A.

The mountain huts below feature in the walks in this guide, either as a lunchtime destination on a circular walk, or in many cases as an overnight stop on one of the two treks

outlined, walked either as a whole or when devising shorter trips.

Cabane d'Essertze (2193m) is a friendly hut with magnificent views, run by the Ski Club Hérémencia. It's about 1hr 30min from Thyon on the Tour du Val d'Hérens (Walk 1).

Cabane de Prafleuri (2656m) is a busy, privately owned hut about 1hr west of the Dixence dam, an important stopover on the Chamonix–Zermatt route, and an alternative to staying at the Hotel du Barrage.

La Cabane des Dix (2928m) is owned by the Monte Rosa section of the SAC. It's a special place to stay, with a real sense of remoteness and rugged beauty, and it's a stopping point for trekkers on the Tour du Val d'Hérens, the Chamonix–Zermatt route and Swiss Route 6.

Cabane des Aiguilles Rouges (2809m) is a friendly hut perched high on the western side of the Val d'Hérens, below the Aiguille Rouge summit, with superb views across the valley and beyond.

Cabane de la Tsa (2606m) is a small private refuge that welcomes walkers, climbers and families. It is easily accessible for a day hike or overnight stay.

Cabane des Becs de Bosson (2982m), with its spectacular 360-degree panoramas, was built by enthusiasts in 1997 on the border of the Val d'Hérens, Val d'Anniviers and Val de Réchy.

Cabane de Moiry (2826m) overlooks the Moiry glacier icefall. The new building houses small dormitories and rooms, the dining room has picture windows overlooking the ice, and the old building has been renovated.

Cabane du Petit Mountet (2140m) sits on the crest of a moraine to the south of Zinal. It's an easy walk to this friendly refuge, either for lunch or an overnight stop. Family friendly, it also features in the TCVA.

Cabane du Grand Mountet (2886m) is a substantial refuge commanding exceptional views. A starting point for mountaineers tackling the Zinalrothorn and Ober Gabelhorn, it's an exciting excursion for more capable walkers, on the TCVA.

Cabane Arpitettaz (2786m) stands at the foot of the Weisshorn and is run by the SAC. Located above the popular Arpitettaz lake, it makes a fine high-altitude overnight stop.

Cabane de Tracuit (3259m) is a modern hut and the highest refuge mentioned in this guidebook. It is often used by mountaineers tackling the 4000m Bishorn and Weisshorn and can be accessed directly from the valley above Zinal, and on a traverse over a col from the Cabane Arpitettaz.

Cabane Bella-Tola (2347m) was renovated in 2021. It's a friendly place providing good restaurant food and accommodation for walkers and mountaineers. It's easily accessible from the St Luc–Tignousa funicular.

There is also the **Hotel Weisshorn (2337m)**, an historic mountain hotel oozing traditional charm – at a price! Daytime refreshments are served on the terrace but note that there are no views of the Weisshorn, although the views down towards the Rhône valley are superb.

Staying in a mountain hut

Visiting one or more mountain huts and, better still, spending a couple of nights up high, should be part of your Swiss mountain walking experience. Take in the views, the sunsets and the sunrises and enjoy the chance to make new friends, new memories and new plans. For many it's a new experience, but it is easy to get the hang of it.

On arrival, change into hut shoes, either the ones provided (crocs or similar) or your own. One of the staff will show you to a dorm or small room, and will usually ask if you have special dietary requests. Sort your bed out early, keep your gear tucked away and tidy, get washing and personal tasks out of the way and then settle back to enjoy the late afternoon and evening. You will be allocated seats for dinner, usually served at 18:00 or 19:00. Settle your bill after dinner. Breakfasts are generally modest and early. Before you depart, leave your bed space tidy, folding bedding, and check you have got all your kit. Huts will also provide picnic lunches for the trail, ask on arrival.

Duvets and pillows are provided, but you will need a sleeping bag liner – silk ones are lighter and more comfortable. Liners can often be rented at the hut, so check when you book. Bedtime is generally before 22:00, when the hut goes quiet and the late-night rustling of plastic bags is to be avoided. Many huts also serve climbers, who may slip out any time after 03:00, depending on their route.

Do book ahead, especially if planning to stay in one of the huts on the Chamonix–Zermatt route (Prafleurie, Cabane des Dix, Cabane de Moiry, Hotel Weisshorn and Cabane Bella-Tola). Huts may be busy and staff need to plan meals in advance. Most hut staff speak some English, but you are likely to find yourself chatting to others in French, sometimes German, and to walkers from around the world. If your plans change, or if you are unable to get to the hut, call to let them know. Failing to arrive at a scheduled hut may lead to a search if you are thought to have gone missing.

Other local facilities

All the larger villages have a range of shops and restaurants, and most have a bank with a cashpoint. There are outdoor stores in Grimentz, Chandolin, St Luc, Zinal, Evolène, Les Haudères and Arolla.

The main hospital is in Sion. Vissoie and Evolène have pharmacies and doctors.

The Ober Gabelhorn from the Cabane du Grand Mountet (Walk 29)

The wild upper section of the Ferpècle valley, with the Dent Blanche on the left (Walk 12)

MAPS

Swiss mapping is excellent and clear. However, it is crucial you buy a Wanderkarte, a map marked with the footpath network – versions without the paths highlighted may be things of beauty, but they are difficult to use for walking.

Recommended maps are as follows:

- Swisstopo 1306 Sion at 1:25,000 covering the lower Val d'Hérens south to just beyond Euseigne. Note this map does not have hiking paths highlighted
- Swisstopo 273T Montana at 1:50,000, 1km = 2cm
- Swisstopo 283T Arolla at 1:50,000, 1km = 2cm
- Together, the two 1:50,000 Swisstopo maps comprise high-quality mapping overlaid with graded hiking paths covering all of both valleys, from Sion and Sierre south and including the Dix valley, but the scale is perhaps a bit big for walking
- Kümmerly+Frey Val d'Anniviers/ Val d'Hérens 23 at 1:60,000 covers the whole area; a match for the Swisstopo in clarity, with additional features. Water resistant
- Hallwag 34: Grimentz, Zinal, Val d'Hérens at 1:50,000 (1km = 2cm) comprises high-quality mapping overlaid with graded hiking paths covering the entire area of both valleys

Map sources are given in Appendix A.

The route maps provided in this guidebook are at 1:50,000, 2cm = 1km. These are derived from open-source data but have been reviewed in detail by the authors. Spellings and heights have been standardised as far as possible against online Swisstopo mapping, but be aware that different maps have a range of heights and that signpost heights and spellings may differ from those on the maps. For your information, we have set the following commonly used heights as follows: Arolla (2008m), Les Haudères (1451m), Evolène (1372m), Zinal (1674m), Grimentz (1564m) and its cable-car station at 1590m.

APPS

In our digital world, apps are a valuable component of the walker's toolkit. The valley is covered by many digital mapping resources, such as Outdooractive and PhoneMaps. The following apps are specifically recommended for the walking visitor.

Mapping – SwitzerlandMobility and Swisstopo apps provide access to all the Swiss mapping databases, in online and offline (downloadable) formats. Different tiles can be selected and bought, but it is crucial to download the footpath layer.

Travel – SBB Mobile is a complete Swiss travel app for trains, buses and connecting cable cars, as well as some other services. The app brings together the entirety of the Swiss public transport system into a seamless whole. It's easy to use, linking with online payments and storing your Half Fare Card as well, thereby automatically accessing half-price fares. Note that if you do have a Half Fare Card, you will need to show a printout when tickets are inspected.

Weather – MeteoSchweiz/MétéoSuisse is a weather app from the Swiss meteorological agency that has full forecasting capabilities. It takes a little time to get the hang of, as it has lots of resources to explore, but it's worth the effort and is a bit more accurate than more general weather apps that may not fully account for Swiss mountain conditions.

PREPARATION

It is much better to be fit before starting a mountain walking holiday. If you are hill fit in your home country, you will have few or no issues. Even a few lower walks will help with your preparation, especially if you manage two or three consecutive days, wearing walking boots and carrying a rucksack; it should assist in your acclimatisation to the higher altitude. At 1600m and 1800m you may feel little effect, but over 2500m the effect of the altitude will kick in, and you should gain height progressively before going far above 3000m. If you develop a headache, the best thing to do is to descend.

EQUIPMENT

Regular hiking gear is all that should be needed for most of these routes. For footwear, light to mid-weight boots are ideal, but many walkers are happy using trainers or approach shoes, provided they have a good tread. Use what you would generally use on a rocky hike.

You may see no rain whatsoever during a two-week holiday, but mountain weather is changeable, so you could experience some rain daily. Late-afternoon thunderstorms are likely to be the main issue. A light to mid-weight jacket and waterproof trousers should be adequate for these routes. Walking poles are a matter of choice, but provide stability on rough and exposed ground. You will also need a 20–30L rucksack to carry your waterproofs, food for the day, spare fleece, hat, gloves, first-aid kit, water, camera, etc.

If you plan to tackle harder or higher routes in early summer, an ice axe and crampons could be a useful addition, assuming you have the space to carry them and the necessary mountaineering experience to use them. If you decide to hire a guide to do a climb, you can also hire the required gear. Likewise, via ferrata protection (harness, lanyard, helmet) is not required unless you want to tackle some of the local via ferratas (see Evolène introduction).

USING THIS GUIDE

This guide provides 35 walking routes split between the Val d'Anniviers, the Moiry valley, Val d'Hérens and the Dix area.

Distance, walking time, ascent and descent for each route are shown, together with a broad grade or indication of difficulty. Access is outlined and the main refreshment opportunities are mentioned.

Walking times

The walking times in this guide are based on the steady pace of a reasonably fit hill/mountain walker and don't allow for stops, lunch, afternoon cake, long siestas or photo sessions, so in practice you will need to adjust these timings to match your own preferences. A 5hr walking day with several long stops might result in 7–8hr on the mountain. Timings will usually agree with the signposted times on the yellow signs throughout the valleys.

You should also consider your fitness and acclimatisation. Even if you are fit, take time to get used to the altitude. If you have had a long flight or journey from abroad, bear in mind that the combined effect of jet lag and altitude can be challenging, throwing all walking times into disarray, so do make allowances in the first few days of a trip and start with some easier routes. In most cases, times that were challenging at the start of a holiday will seem much easier by the end of a week or two.

Grades of paths

Swiss paths are graded into three levels of path:

- **Hiking trails** (*chemins pédestres*) don't place any particular demands on the walker. They are marked on the ground in yellow or with yellow diamonds (not to be confused with the signposts, which are also yellow).

- **Mountain hiking trails** (*chemins de randonnée de montagne*) require walkers to be sure-footed, unafraid of heights, physically fit and experienced in the mountains. They are signposted with red-and-white waymarks or pointers on the yellow signposts.
- **Alpine trails** (*chemins de randonnée alpine*) demand that users are sure-footed, unafraid of heights and physically very fit; alpine experience and additional mountain equipment may be required. The paths are marked with blue-and-white waymarks or blue signs.

Most paths are well graded. Yellow paths are easy; blue paths are hard. Red-and-white paths, the mountain hiking trails, cover a wide range of walking, so we have provided a more nuanced grading structure (see table).

Gradings used in this guide
Grade 1
An easy walk, mainly on undemanding yellow paths or tracks, but likely with some red-and-white sections, in the valley or just above.
Grade 2
A moderate walk on clear and mainly straightforward mountain paths with no significant exposure or problematic ground; however, the route may be long with considerable up and down and an occasional rail or steps.

Grade 3
A harder mountain walk on higher red-and-white mountain paths situated further away from valley bases and habitation. Ascents, descents and walk times will be long, and in places there may be trickier ground, exposure and aided sections (cables, steps, ladders).
Grade 4
A high, hard mountain walk, usually taking in parts of the blue alpine trail. Considerable ascent and descent will be involved, the ground will be rough and rocky, there may be exposed passages and there will probably be sections aided with cables, steps and ladders.

Bear in mind that a route is given a grade as a whole, so there may be an occasional harder section on a Grade 2 route, and a Grade 4 may have substantial sections of easier walking.

It's important to note that as snow and ice on mountain slopes melts and ice on mountain slopes melts, landslides can occur and paths can become damaged by subsidence from below or stonefall from above, so take account of path conditions as you find them and alter your plans accordingly. Online Swisstopo/SwitzerlandMobility mapping will show any paths that are closed.

The Col de Riedmatten and the Pas de Chèvres
The passage from the Lac des Dix to Arolla is over one of two passes – the Col de Riedmatten or the Pas de Chèvres (goats). Both are the main

A typical Swiss signpost showing red-and-white mountain hiking routes, local routes and the Tour du Val Hérens

route of the Chamonix–Zermatt Walkers Haute Route trek.

Riedmatten at 2919m is a steep shaly notch with some cables, a stern pull with one step back for every two steps forward. It is safe but some will find it hard and exposed. This has now been co-opted by Swiss walking route 6 so has become the main crossing point.

The Pas de Chèvres is slightly lower at 2855m and renowned for its series of ladders which since replacement some years ago are solid and well protected. But the route to the ladders is across eroded, rocky ground and has deteriorated and become a difficult section for the normal walker. There are plans to improve this in spring 2024 so the route may become easier and safer. Check locally, either with the guardian at the Cabane des Dix or the guides office by the sports shop in Arolla for the latest information.

GPX tracks

GPX tracks for the routes in this guidebook are available to download free at www.cicerone.co.uk/1096/GPX.

A GPS device is an excellent aid to navigation, but you should also carry a map and compass and know how to use them. GPX files are provided in good faith, but neither the authors nor the publisher accepts responsibility for their accuracy.

ESSENTIAL TERMS
alpage mountain pasture
barrage dam
bisse irrigation channel
buvette snack bar
cabane refuge
difficile difficult
passerelle suspension bridge

Up close to the Euseigne pyramids – the conglomerate structure is clearly seen (Walk 18)

Looking back down to the Tsa ridge across the valley from Arolla (Walk 4)

The Val d'Hérens remains one of the most undeveloped and traditional Swiss valleys. Farming is supported and respected as are family traditions and national dress, particularly on special occasions. Despite its insular and off-the-beaten-track feel, the valley is home to the famous sturdy black Hérens cows, a breed well adapted to the high pastures and known for its fighting capabilities (although generally docile), and the Arolla pine, a shorter, more verdant version of the many Pinus species, which is found on higher mountain slopes across Europe.

The villages are a delight. Within the main eastern branch, the old village of Evolène is the largest and is recognised as one of Switzerland's most beautiful. A short distance up valley, Les Haudères has fine old timber houses, while at the valley head at 2000m Arolla comprises a few hotels, shops and the highest campsite in the Alps, and is the start point for many of the higher routes. Development throughout the valley is slow and modest, in character with the traditional buildings.

The way up from Sion into the Val d'Hérens climbs steep hillsides carved by the river Borgne, and near Euseigne, famous for its calcified pyramids, the valley splits into two, the main branch to the east, and the Val d'Hérémence, carved by the river Dixence to the west. The traditional villages in the main branch of the valley have largely resisted development as ski resorts, with just one small chairlift from Evolène and limited seasonal lifts above Arolla. The mountains are all under the 4000m level; Mont Collon (3637m), Pigne d'Arolla (3781m) and Mont Blanc de Cheilon (3870m) are fine mountains with easier mountaineering routes, and Arolla has traditionally been an ideal base for a first alpine season. With its tumbling glaciers, the Dent Blanche (4357m) is the highest in the area and dominates the Evolène skyline yet hides away above the Ferpècle valley.

The western branch splits off near Euseigne and leads south into the Hérémence valley and the Dixence barrage, the principal part of a major water-management and power-generation scheme serving the whole of Switzerland. Above the substantial dam and lake, the Cabane des Dix and the diminished glaciers of Mont Blanc de Cheilon are easily accessible to walkers, with paths linking to the Val d'Hérens.

The Tour du Val d'Hérens is a six-day route forming a horseshoe tour between Thyon and Nax, visiting remote mountain refuges and traditional villages while trekking through the Val d'Hérémence, Dix area and Val d'Hérens.

Val d'Hérémence (Dix)

WALK 1

Thyon to Grande Dixence barrage

Start	Thyon (2096m)
Finish	Hotel du Barrage 'the Ritz!' (2138m)
Distance	17.5km
Total ascent	780m
Total descent	740m
Grade	2
Time	6hr
Max altitude	2411m at building above the barrage
Refreshments	Cabane d'Essertze (2193m)
Access	Bus services to Thyon, and from Hotel du Barrage (Le Chargeur). Gondola lift from Veysonnaz

This walk traverses high above the western side of the Hérémence valley, much of it undulating at or around 2200m. It's a beautiful walk above the treeline, the hillsides covered with bilberry and alpenrose, with superb views throughout. The friendly Cabane d'Essertze is reached after about 2hr, beyond which there is a great feeling of remoteness.

Thyon is not the most attractive starting point for a walk – a purpose-built ski village, deserted during the summer months. However, an early morning bus service from Vex provides ample time for the entire walk, with a bus return from the barrage. This route is also Stage 1 of the Tour du Val d'Hérens, with a continuation to Arolla and beyond (or via the Dix hut) the next day (See Walks 2 and 3).

Walk up the main entrance steps into the 'village' and follow yellow diamond waymarkers to the left of the information office, diagonally across the main square, then between buildings and down steps to a large parking area. A signpost on the far left leads up a track. Branch left at a right-hand bend onto an unsigned

sonnaz

Forêt de Magrappé

Les Collons

Thyon 2096m

S ◻ Thyon 2096m

Hérémence

Thyon cable-car station ■

La Mura

Aver

206

Prolin

Cerise

Riod

Mont Rouge ▲ 2490m

2381m
2366m

Mâche

Les Gouilles

Cabane d'Essertze 2193m

▲ Greppon Blanc 2713m

N

Bec de a Montau ▲ 2922m

0   1
━━━━━━━━━━ km

■ L'Orchère 2098m

Map continues on page 42

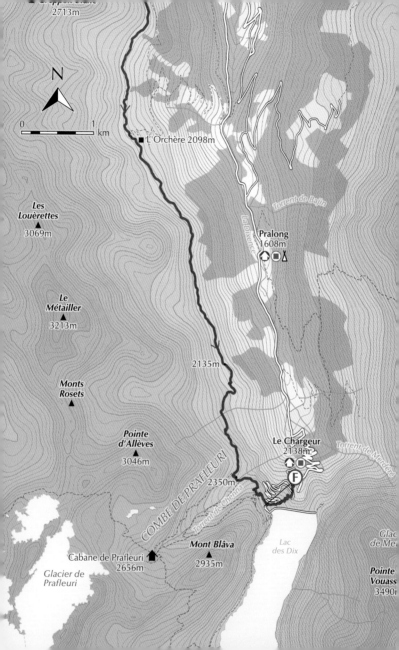

N

0   1
|___|___|___|___| km

Pignn Blanc
2713m

L'Orchère 2098m

Les
Louèrettes
3069m

Le
Métailler
3213m

Monts
Rosets

Pointe
d'Allèves
3046m

Torrent de Bajin

Pralong
1608m

La Dixence

2135m

2350m

COMBE DE PRAFLEURI

Le Chargeur
2138m

Torrent de Merdera

F

Torrent de Chenna

Cabane de Prafleuri
2656m

Mont Blâva
2935m

Lac
des Dix

Glacier de
Prafleuri

Glac
de Me

Pointe
Vouass
3490m

path across a hillside covered in bilberries, pass under the Trabanta chairlift and keep on a rising path to a junction at 2179m. Continue straight across, climbing again, then fork right onto a track which narrows to a path rising to a small col at **2381m** (1hr 15min).

Views up the valley are tremendous, and down to the attractive lakes of **Les Gouilles d'Essertze**. This area is of special scientific interest, as the natural lakes, interspersed with coarse grasses and areas of bog, are over 13,000 years old.

Descend and follow the path to the east (left) of the lakes, then fork left above the second (Rion) lake, crossing the huge grassy bowl to a junction and another lake. Turn left to follow the grassy track as it descends between peat bogs, turning right to pass a large dairy farm, and then continue on a gravel track to the **Cabane d'Essertze** (2193m, 2hr). This welcoming refuge is the only place offering refreshments on the route.

Take the path (or continue on the track) from the hut following green TVH signs, then after 250m take the grassy track up to the right. This quickly turns into a path tracing a superb balcony route across a hillside filled with bilberries and alpenrose. The path undulates slightly from time to time, passes above a large farm at **L'Orchère** and crosses two or three short sections of boulders to reach a junction with a rising path (**2135m**, 3hr 15min).

The path now climbs around a rocky promontory then continues up across a large pasture area, grazed by sheep protected by guard dogs, to a small col (2350m, 5hr).

Dogs guarding sheep (**patous**) can be intimidating if they spot you and approach. Keep calm and let them confirm you are not a threat to the flock. Refer to guidance in 'The walking' in the Introduction on how to react if they move towards you.

Now descend into the Combe de Prafleuri and cross the **Torrent de Chenna**. If diverting to the Cabane de Prafleuri, turn right here and climb the 2km to the hut. To continue on the route, follow signs for the barrage and climb steeply to pop out at an old wooden building. Take the path just beyond this, descending in tight zigzags, then traverse across to a large flat area, where there are climbing routes up the dam wall, and the end point of a zipwire. You can either climb up the ramp to take the cable car down to the Hotel du Barrage or continue to follow pedestrian signs down a steep, tortuous route, past a tiny chapel, to the hotel and bus stop a little below. **Le Chargeur** (2138m, 6hr).

Pointe de Vouasson dominates the head of the valley, the Dix dam visible below

LA GRANDE DIXENCE

The Grande Dixence is the largest gravity dam in the world. It stands at an impressive 285m high and weighs in the region of 15 million tonnes – more than the Great Pyramid of Giza. A gravity dam is constructed by superimposing concrete blocks on top of each other like a giant drystone wall. This allows for movement, minimising the risk of cracking from seismic activity. The top of the dam can move outwards by up to 14cm when the lake is at capacity. The Lac des Dix is the largest in Switzerland, holding 400 billion litres of water. The first, smaller dam was built between 1929 and 1935, but demand for electricity soared after 1945, so the current dam was constructed between 1950 and 1965. Nearly 100km of underground canals collect meltwater from the surrounding glaciers, as far away as Zermatt, and store it in interconnected reservoirs supplying three power stations. There is a visitor centre at the base of the dam, and guided tours take place between 10:00 and 16:30 inside the dam. For more information and booking, visit www.grande-dixence.ch.

WALK 2

Grande Dixence barrage to Cabane des Dix

Start	Hotel du Barrage (2138m)
Finish	Cabane des Dix (2928m)
Distance	12.5km
Total ascent	900m
Total descent	110m
Grade	2–3
Time	5hr
Max altitude	2956m on col below Tête Noire
Refreshments	None on route
Access	Bus service from Vex to Barrage

This route is one of two halves. Having climbed (or taken the cable car) to the dam wall, enjoy an easy, if long, lakeside walk to the end of the Lac des Dix. A steep climb up the Pas du Chat then enters a high and remote glacial region looking down onto braided glacial outflow streams and lakes and up along a moraine towards the glaciers cascading down from Mont Blanc de Cheilon. The welcoming and atmospheric Cabane des Dix is a memorable place to stay before either returning to the barrage (a 4hr walk) or continuing to Arolla or Evolène as part of Stage 2 of the Tour du Val d'Hérens (see Walk 3).

From the Hotel du Barrage, walk up the steep path behind the hotel to reach the dam wall (35min), or take the cable car. Take the track leading along the right side of the lake, passing through a series of **tunnels** under the rocky promontory below Mont Blâva. (The tunnels are either short or well illuminated; however, a headtorch would be a good idea.)

Having passed through the final tunnel, continue beside the lake, passing a sign up to Col des Roux, with the roof of Refuge La Barme just visible, and the summit of the Pointe de Vouasson (3490m) high above the lake on the other side. At the end of the lake, cross a bridge then turn left to pass under steep rocks to reach a signpost for **Pas du Chat** (2370m, 3hr).

Climb steeply to height 2544m where a thin path joins from the right. The gradient eases as the path continues across rough, rocky terrain, crosses a stream, then begins to climb up onto a moraine. Pass a turn signed left towards the Pas de

Looking north from part way around Lac des Dix, Pic d'Artsinol in the background

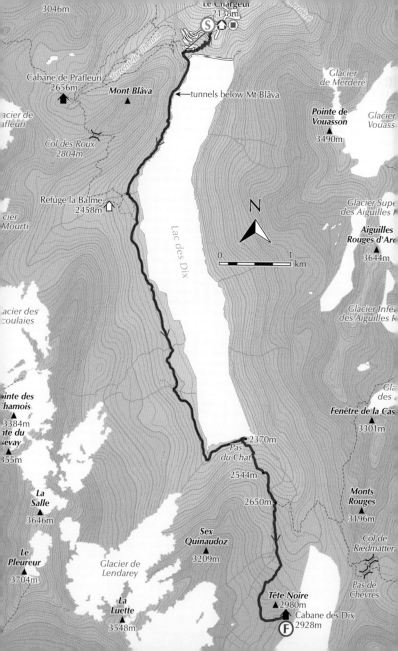

Le Chargeur
2138m

Cabane de Prafleuri
2656m

Mont Blâva

tunnels below Mt Blâva

Col des Roux
2804m

Refuge la Balme
2458m

Lac des Dix

3046m

Glacier
de Merdéré

Pointe de
Vouasson
3490m

Glacier
Vouass

Glacier Supé
des Aiguilles

Aiguilles
Rouges d'Ar
3644m

N

0   1
km

Glacier Infé
des Aiguilles

inte des
hamois
3384m
te du
sevay
355m

La
Salle
3646m

Le
Pleureur
3704m

Glacier de
Lendarey

La
Luette
3548m

Sex
Quinaudoz
3209m

2370m
Pas
du Chat
2544m

2650m

Tête Noire
2980m

Cabane des Dix
2928m

F

Fenêtre de la Cas
3301m

Monts
Rouges
3196m

Col de
Riedmatter

Pas de
Chèvres

Gla
des

Views of the Lac des Dix from the tunnels below Mont Blâva

Chèvres and Col de Riedmatten at approximately **2650m** (Walk 3). If you want to follow the TVH route directly to Arolla over one of the cols, turn left here.

Continue onto the crest of the moraine, with increasingly dramatic views all around, the Tête Noire looming ahead and the north face of Mont Blanc de Cheilon (milk pail) above. A further path off to the left is signed to Arolla, but continue on the moraine, then turn down to the right signed very clearly for the Dix hut (4hr 30min).

The path rises across more rough ground, then in steep zigzags to reach the col just to the right of the **Tête Noire**. The Cabane des Dix can now be seen below, standing on its own small hill behind Tête Noire. Descend from the col and take the path leading directly to the **Cabane des Dix** (2928m, 5hr).

CABANE DES DIX

Cabane des Dix has long been a key starting point for mountaineers attempting climbs on Mont Blanc de Cheilon and La Luette, and on the winter Haute Route ski tour. The main Glacier de Cheilon cascades in icefalls each side of Mont Blanc de Cheilon and, at its greatest extent, created the huge valley between Tête Noire and the two passes leading to Arolla. The glacier has now drastically receded, and the direct route from the Pas de Chèvres to the Cabane des Dix, still shown on some maps, is no longer passable in summer. The icefalls from Mont Blanc de Cheilon are tinged pink with algae, while rock debris now covers most of the lower glacier, sure signs of a dying glacier.

WALK 3
Cabane des Dix to Arolla

Start	Cabane des Dix (2928m)
Finish	Arolla (2008m)
Distance	12.5km
Total ascent	460m
Total descent	1380m
Grade	3
Time	4hr 30min
Max altitude	2956m on col below Tête Noire
Refreshments	Les Chottes buvette above Arolla
Access	Reach the Cabane des Dix by walking from the Dixence barrage. Bus to and from Arolla to Evolène and down valley

This route is designed principally as a continuation of Walk 2. While most of the route is on good mountain paths, there are two passes over to the Val d'Hérens and Arolla – both difficult. The climb to the Col de Riedmatten is short but very loose and steep. Many will find it exposed, the route climbing in tight turns then directly to the top with a chain for protection. The ladders element of the Pas de Chèvres is well maintained; however, during 2023 access was classified as dangerous, as the moraine has collapsed. We understand that improvements allowing a safer passage are anticipated **(Check locally at the guides office/shop in Arolla or the Dix hut before attempting)**.

The continuing path crosses the outwash area at the snout of the Glacier de Cheilon, then climbs onto a lateral moraine leading to the two cols. The route is clear and the way down to Arolla is beautiful, passing the Tsijiore Nouve icefall, and with a good chance of seeing both ibex and chamois.

Leave the Cabane des Dix, fork right to climb back to the col beneath the Tête Noire, then descend to reach easier ground before climbing onto the moraine. The path follows the crest of the moraine to reach a signed path junction at **2650m** (45min). This rejoins the main TVH route.

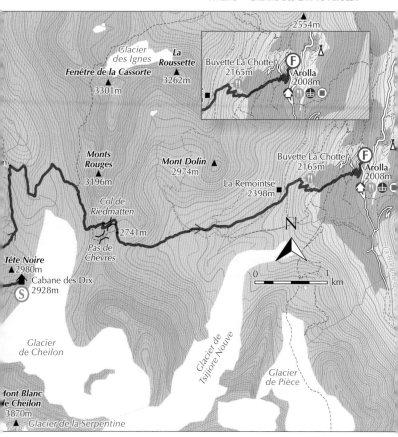

Turn right off the moraine, then rise round a rocky buttress, cross an almost flat outwash area and then climb again onto a lateral moraine leading to the two passes. The route is very well signed with red-and-white paint splashes. Leave the moraine to pass tightly under a rock wall to reach the foot of the Col de Riedmatten (2hr 15min).

The way to the Pas de Chèvres continues ahead but may not be open. It runs below the cliffs, crossing an exposed, dangerous area to reach the ladders. A good

51

Cabane des Dix on its isolated hill, the lower slopes of Mont Blanc de Cheilon on the right

clear path descends from the pass to join the junction with the Riedmatten path at 2741m.

The path to Col de Riedmatten climbs very steeply in tight turns, threading between boulders, then crossing left to reach a section protected with a chain, then continuing to the right into the narrowing cleft also protected by a chain, leading a few minutes later to the **Col de Riedmatten** (2918m, 2hr 30min).

The **view** from the top of both passes is fantastic, across to the distinctive Aiguille de la Tsa (Tza), with the Dent de Perroc to the left and the perfect triangle of the Dent Blanche behind; and from the Pas de Chèvres (and a little lower below the Col de Riedmatten), the Matterhorn can be seen in the far distance.

From the Col de Riedmatten, descend on a good path, looking out for chamois and ibex. The path from the Pas de Chèvres joins from the right at the **2741m**

junction. Continue down fairly steeply for a while, then as the gradient eases enjoy good views up to the right to the Tsijiore Nouve icefall, and Mont Collon at the head of the Arolla valley. Cross a small bridge at 2538m and continue descending to reach a small group of derelict chalets at **La Remointse** (2398m, 3hr 30min).

Take the path down to the right, then at a hairpin bend turn right and descend in a series of zigzags to reach the seasonal **Buvette La Chotte** (2165m, 4hr).

To continue to Arolla, descend the track, then take the signed path to the right down through pine woods to reach the Grand Hotel & Kurhaus. Turn left then right to continue down the road and into the central square and bus terminus at **Arolla** (2008m, 4hr 30min).

From **Arolla** the TVH continues more gently down valley (see Walk 9). Arolla has a range of hotels, food and outdoor shops and refreshments, as well as buses down the valley.

The wild scenery between the Lac des Dix and the Pas de Chèvres

Arolla

WALK 4
Pas de Chèvres from Arolla

Start/finish	Arolla (2008m)
Distance	11.5km
Total ascent	860m
Total descent	860m
Grade	2
Time	4hr 30min (2hr 50min in ascent; 1hr 40min on the descent)
Max altitude	2854m on the Pas de Chèvres
Refreshments	La Chotte buvette at 2165m, 30min above Arolla
Access	Bus to Arolla

The walk to the Pas de Chèvres is a classic of the valley. It is an excellent route with a straightforward path climbing above the hamlet of Arolla to the fine col, with wonderful views. It is also likely that you will see wildlife – chamois and ibex higher up and marmots throughout the climb.

From Arolla Poste, take the road uphill and continue on the path at the first hairpin. Climb broad zigzags to the Grand Hotel & Kurhaus (2068m, 10min) and take the path as it rises above the frankly enormous but discretely sited hotel. This section is criss-crossed by woodland paths, but the heavily rooted main path climbs to a track (20min). Turn left on the track and come to the buvette of **La Chotte** (2165m, 30min).

Immediately after the buvette, find the path that climbs the grassy hillside in numerous broad zigzags, many with cut-throughs that are best avoided. Pass a rise with a bench and continue to the abandoned buildings of **La Remointse** (2398m, 1hr 10min). Pass under a small ski tow as the path levels out. Continue to a bridge and briefly join a track before heading up to the left (2538m, 1hr 40min).

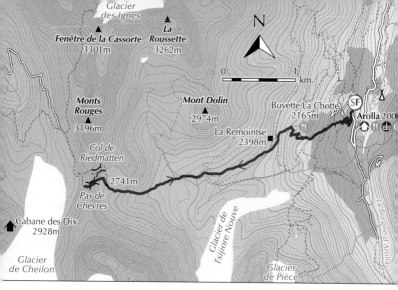

Climb more steeply on a rougher path. At **2741m** reach a junction with the Col de Riedmatten signed right (see below) and the Pas de Chèvres left. Climb to the **Pas de Chèvres** (2854m, 2hr 40min).

> The **view from the col** is spectacular. Below is the Glacier de Cheilon with the Cabane des Dix perched high on rocks directly across. Down valley is the Lac des Dix, while up valley is the north face of Mont Blanc de Cheilon at 3870m, just missing out on the 4000m status. To the east is the rock wall of the Veisivi–Tsa range, which continues south to the Italian border. Peering over these is the Dent Blanche, and the slender spike of the Matterhorn is also clearly visible above the ridge. Directly ahead are the col's famous ladders; they are robust with platforms but might still cause jitters for those with no head for heights.

Options from the Pas de Chèvres

The route to the ladders on the Dix side is difficult on a crumbling moraine under the rock face below. It may be closed. **Check locally at the guides office/shop in Arolla or the Dix hut before attempting.** Options from here are as follows:

- Descend the ladders (which are strong and as protected as possible but need a sound head for heights). Carefully cross the rough moraine under the cliffs to join the Riedmatten path (Walk 3). If this route is open, keep strictly to the marked route close to the cliffs and do not stray into the turbulent moraine.

The Upper Arolla valley and Mont Collon seen on the descent route, showing the route to Plan Bertol and the Italian border

- Reverse down to the 2741m Riedmatten junction and climb to the col (30min). Views here are restricted. Carefully descend the steep slope – initially protected by chains but soon an 'interesting', awkward but manageable descent to the path below – returning up the ladders.
- From the Col de Riedmatten, reverse Walk 3 to the Cabane des Dix in 2hr 30min or descend to the Lac des Dix and barrage, taking 3hr 30min (reversing Walk 2).

Return to Arolla
To return to Arolla, reverse the route allowing 2hr for a relaxed descent. If the buvette isn't open, there are several cafés in **Arolla** (2008m, 4hr 30min).

WALK 5

Cabane des Aiguilles Rouges from Arolla

Start/finish	Arolla poste (2008m)
Distance	13.5km
Total ascent	1100m (820m on the ascent to the cabane)
Total descent	1100m
Grade	3
Time	5hr 45min (2hr 45min on the ascent to the cabane)
Max altitude	2845m just after the Cabane des Aiguilles Rouges
Refreshments	Cabane des Aiguilles Rouges and seasonal buvette at Lac Bleu
Access	Bus to Arolla

The Cabane des Aiguilles Rouges is the start point for many climbs in the Aiguilles Rouges range, and it is also a fine destination in its own right, whether for a night in the hut or a day walk. The route climbs from Arolla to the alpage (mountain pasture) of Pragra, and then takes an intricate but well-crafted route through glacial debris to the hut. The descent is steep but comes to the idyllic Lac Bleu, the route finishing along the high trail marked 'chemin difficile' and ending in Arolla.

From the central hairpin in Arolla, head past the sports shop. At the first hairpin continue on the path, which itself makes hairpins. At the fourth, just before the vast **Grand Hotel & Kurhaus**, head uphill on the road (the Route des Marmottes) and at the first turn continue straight on (not currently signed except for the Sentier des Marmottes boards) (15min).

Take the path ahead which climbs past trees and comes into a hillside of open land and pasture; the Pragra buildings sit at the top of this. Here the path interlaces with farm tracks but look out for the yellow signs that mark the way. Climb the hillside, joining with and leaving the tracks several times, to eventually arrive at the **Remointse de Pragra** (2476m, 1hr 20min).

Alpine farms, of which Pragra is a fine example, make for a hard life, even with modern transport. The herd is brought up from the valley, or further

afield, each spring (transhumance) and lives at the high pasture until the end of the summer grass, usually late August or early September, when the process is reversed.

After exploring the buildings (and perhaps buying some of the cheese), continue climbing gradually. After 10min, pass a turn to a viewpoint at Le Troûco. This detour takes 20min there and back, but it's a fine viewpoint above the whole valley and the Tsa range on the far side.

Soon the path enters an intricate section as it crosses glacial debris, streams and piles of rocks. Climb and descend several times. The path crosses boulders which seem to be fortunately laid out to assist the walker. After climbing a short section of moraine with drops to the right, enter a rockier section, where it is best to keep lower to refind the waymarked path. Blue marks on rocks identify the start of the Col des Ignes alpine path to the Dix valley; do not follow these.

The hillside may have looked uncrossable from afar but close up the path is good and makes an almost level crossing of the boulder-filled slopes. One awkward section across a rock face is assisted by chains and a ladder and looks more awkward than it actually is. Continue to climb steadily to reach the **Cabane des Aiguilles Rouges** (2809m, 2hr 45min).

The **Cabane des Aiguilles Rouges** is the start point for many rock climbs in the Aiguilles Rouges range above, as well as winter ski tours. It is owned by the Geneva section of the SAC and has dormitory places for 80.

Steps and chains assist the walker across a buttress on the way to the Cabane des Aiguilles Rouges

The Cabane des Aiguilles Rouges (photo David Dear)

Leave the hut and continue to climb for a couple of minutes. The routes above the hut even 20 years ago were easy snow climbs, now they are stony trails. Pass a sculpture of the same series as those sited around Arolla. There is a small lake that dries out in late summer.

Drop steeply down the moraine to a river crossing (with a good footbridge) and continue to descend less steeply over rocky ground that becomes grassy. There are glimpses of Lac Bleu far below, and the cabane is in view for most of the descent. After 1hr from the hut, pass a substantial cross with views up and down the valley. Continue the descent and arrive at **Lac Bleu** (2091m, 4hr 15min).

> A **seasonal buvette** is located just below the outflow of the lake. Options from Lac Bleu include the normal descent to La Gouille for buses and a café (30min), or you can take the lower-level route back to Arolla (see Walk 6). The route described takes the higher, more direct path, the so-called 'chemin difficile'.

From the outflow, and facing the lake, climb left, south, over a small rise. Drop down to a bridge and keep right at a path junction (left is the easier, lower return path). The chemin rises and falls, takes in five short sections of cable and continues to traverse into Arolla. Pop out, almost literally, opposite the Hotel du Glacier. Turn right for other facilities and buses in **Arolla** (2008m, 5hr 45min).

WALK 6
Lac Bleu circular walk from Arolla

Start/finish	Arolla village centre (2008m)
Distance	9.5km
Total ascent	540m
Total descent	540m
Grade	2
Time	3hr 45min
Max altitude	2122m just above Lac Bleu
Refreshments	Buvette at lake; cafés/restaurants at La Gouille and Arolla
Access	Bus to Arolla

This is a circular walk to one of the best beauty spots in the area. Busy on sunny days, you will rarely have Lac Bleu to yourself, but by doing a circular walk you may find quieter moments. The walk up to the lake is mostly through a hillside of pine and mixed woodland. The descent to La Gouille follows a wide path through woods, the route finishing with a riverside path and a suspension bridge before returning to Arolla.

The walk can be shortened by starting and finishing at Pramoûss (bus stop), saving a total of about 1hr and 170m of ascent and descent.

From the Poste in Arolla walk down Rue de l'Évêque towards the Hotel du Glacier and take the signed path to the left up some small steps. Initially steep, the path levels as it passes below a large building and then rises more steadily again. After 10min fork right where a path to the left is signed as difficile. This is an alternative route (the 'chemin difficile') to Lac Bleu (see below). The path is sometimes muddy, descending through mixed woodland, with occasional views down into the valley, to join a track just above the road opposite the hamlet of **Pramoûss** (1837m, 35min).

Turn left onto the track and then left at a bend, now signed to Louché Lac Bleu. The woodland path rises immediately, and views into the valley and ahead entice you forwards. After a brief section where the path is less steep, the final zigzag section brings you to a junction with the higher (difficile) path (1hr 30min).

The 'chemin difficile' option

Turn left up the path signed 'chemin difficile', which immediately becomes rockier. The 'difficile' is arguably exaggerated so don't be deterred; its label is

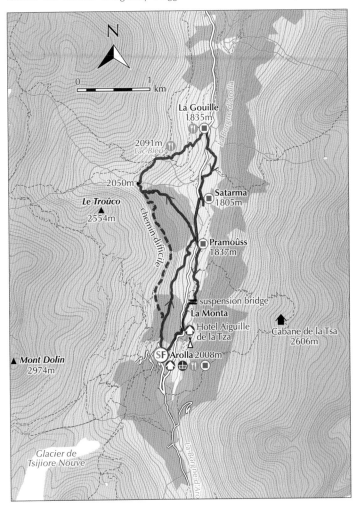

Lac Bleu

designed to put off the inexperienced – but it does have a section of Grade 3 path traversing steep ground high above the valley.

The first half of the route trends uphill and the second half downhill, but there is nearly 350m of up and 250m of down between Arolla and Lac Bleu, so it is undulating all the way. Come to the first chain section after 35min; there are five sections, all short and the chains are perhaps more reassuring than necessary. Cross two bridges over a stream after 1hr 5min (2050m) and join the main route. The 'chemin difficile' is likely to be slightly quicker than the main route.

Main route

Turn right, cross a stream at **2050m** in a large gully, then after a short climb come to open pasture looking down onto **Lac Bleu** (2091m, 1hr 45min).

> **Lac Bleu** is situated in an ideal location – high enough that views up to Mont Collon and the surrounding mountains are spectacular – and on a fine day the water is certainly an intense blue. A path goes around the lake, and there is a small buvette just below. The views across to the Veisivi–Tsa range are tremendous but hide the even bigger mountains to the east.

Take the broader but steep, descending path past the buvette and continue through woodland in numerous zigzags, probably passing countless people on their way up, to arrive at **La Gouille** (1835m, 2hr 25min, refreshments, bus stop).

Leaving La Gouille, turn right and walk along the road for about 100m, then take the steep path down on the left to cross a bridge over the Borgne d'Arolla river. Follow the grassy track over meadows then recross the river to walk through the tiny hamlet of **Satarma** (1805m, 2hr 40min).

Rejoin the road then take a further path down on the left to cross the river. Staying at the same height as the river, follow the path over sand and gravel (take care in periods when the river is full), then climb briefly to reach a cluster of buildings at **Pramoûss** (1837m, 3hr). Cross the river for buses up and down the valley road.

The path continues near the river, then climbs briefly to the 75m suspension bridge: a marvellous Himalayan-style bridge with very little 'wobble'. Cross the bridge, with great views up and down the valley, and pass between chalets and barns at La Monta to reach **Hotel Aiguille de la Tza** (3hr 20min).

Walk up to the main road, cross straight over, then follow the rising woodland path to pass just below the Hotel du Glacier and into **Arolla** (2008m, 3hr 45min).

The substantial Hotel de la Tsa just below Arolla is convenient for the campsite

WALK 7

Plan Bertol from Arolla

Start/finish	Arolla (2008m)
Distance	12km
Total ascent	750m (700m on the climb)
Total descent	750m
Grade	3
Time	4hr 30min (2hr 30min on the climb)
Max altitude	2664m at Plan Bertol
Refreshments	None on the route
Access	Bus to Arolla

Looking out on Mont Collon and its glaciers, Plan Bertol is a small, high and level pasture with an unmanned safety refuge. It sits on the route to the Cabane de Bertol and on the Tour of the Matterhorn (Cervin) route into Italy, which is crossed on the glaciated Col Collon. The extent of damage to glaciers is illustrated by the almost total disappearance of the Upper Arolla glacier.

Bertol was a key site in the construction of the glacial feeds into the Dix dam in the 1950s; indeed a whole village was built to support workers at 2300m, but this has since been almost completely eradicated.

From Arolla Poste, head down the road and straight ahead at the road's first hairpin. Pass the informal parking and continue up the track, passing the left turn over a bridge for the Cabane de la Tsa, then the Arolla pumping station on the right.

Water for the Dix dam is collected from across the southern Valais, as far away as Zermatt and Saas-Fee. The **Arolla pumping station**, the largest of the network, takes water from the Mont Collon and Ferpècle valleys and lifts it from the riverbed, at about 2000m, to the Dix reservoir at 2400m. See Walk 1 for notes on the whole Dix network.

Continue on the track. The track crosses a **bridge** over the riverbed (2090m, 45min). Take the track to the right. After a few twists and turns, take the mountain

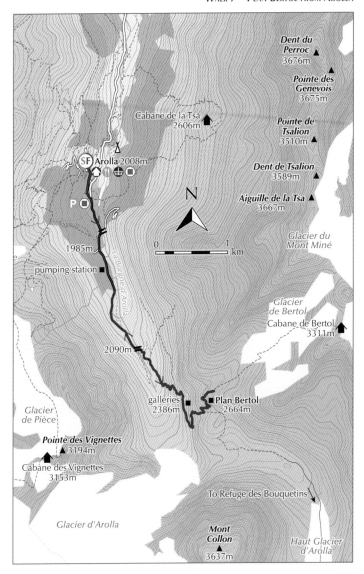

Dent du
Perroc ▲
3676m

Pointe des
Genevois ▲
3675m

Cabane de la Tsa ▲
2606m

Pointe de
Tsalion ▲
3510m

Dent de Tsalion ▲
3589m

Arolla 2008m

Aiguille de la Tsa ▲
3667m

Glacier du
Mont Miné

P

N

0   1 km

1985m

pumping station ▪

Glacier
de Bertol
Cabane de Bertol ▲
3311m

2090m

galleries ▪ ▪ Plan Bertol
2386m   2664m

Glacier
de Pièce

Pointe des Vignettes
▲ 3194m

Cabane des Vignettes ▲
3153m

To Refuge des Bouquetins ↘

Glacier d'Arolla

Mont
Collon
▲
3637m

Haut Glacier
d'Arolla

67

path signed to Plan Bertol and the higher cabanes. Climb steadily on a good path and at 2350m carefully cross an eroded stream bed and come out on a moraine path. At **2386m** (1hr 30min) find a bench near galleries in the rock face, the site of the village created for the dam construction.

From here the path gets more demanding. Climb above the flat area, then steeply into a stony gully. A path to the right (which can be taken on the descent) eventually leads towards the Refuge des Bouquetins far to the south, but keep left and climb a series of long zigzags crafted into the pile of stones that forms the hillside. In fact, the path is as good as it could be in the circumstances, etched into the steep and difficult hillside. Be sure you are happy reversing it later. As you continue to climb, the path levels out and emerges at **Plan Bertol** (2664m, 2hr 30min).

To return to the valley, reverse the ascent route, taking care on the potentially exposed and eroded upper path. Turn right at the bridge and continue into Arolla. The route passes informative information boards about the vast Dix network and water collection through Arolla. Arrive in **Arolla** (2008m, 4hr 30min plus any extra time exploring onward from Plan Bertol).

The upper Arolla glacier – the route taken by the Tour of the Matterhorn into Italy

Looking up to the Glacier de Bertol to the cabane (right of centre) at 3300m

PLAN BERTOL

Plan Bertol comprises a rough pasture. There is also a small building which is open but there are no services; it's purely for safety at this important spot.

Plan Bertol is a crossroads. For an alternative route down, head south then turn right, descending to the path junction above the stone gulley seen earlier. For those with mountaineering capability (and crampons and an axe), the climb to the Cabane de Bertol at 3311m at the head of the Glacier de Bertol is feasible. It's mainly over rubble, but with sections on the glacier. For walkers, the 40min climb to the snout of the glacier is straightforward and confirms that the climb beyond to the cabane deserves care.

Heading south, a path drops to the place where the upper Arolla glacier used to be. The vast mountains of rock left by the glacier are the dominating feature of the valley. The unmanned Refuge des Bouquetins is about 1hr away. The onward route crosses the upper glacier to the Col de Collon into Italy on the Tour of the Matterhorn.

WALK 8
Cabane de la Tsa from Arolla

Start/finish	Arolla Poste (2008m)
Distance	9.5km
Total ascent	860m (675m on the climb to the Cabane)
Total descent	860m
Grade	2
Time	4hr (2hr on the climb to the cabane)
Max altitude	2606m at the Cabane de la Tsa
Refreshments	Cabane de la Tsa, Hotel Aiguille de la Tza and Arolla
Access	Bus to Arolla

This walk is a great introduction to the area. Climbing high above Arolla on the opposite side of the valley, it gives extensive views of the Pigne d'Arolla, the Pas de Chèvres, the mountains beyond the Cabane des Dix and the Aiguilles Rouges across the valley, as well as a close look at the Aiguille de la Tsa and its neighbouring rock climbers' peaks. A welcoming hut with refreshments at the halfway point helps make it a fine outing. If there is snow lying on the boulder field just after the hut, the grade of the route should be classed as being a level higher. In this case you may prefer to descend the way you came up.

In reverse – allow 2hr 30min to reach the hut. Note that the spellings 'Tsa' and 'Tza' seem to be used interchangeably.

From the centre of Arolla, head down the road to the first hairpin. (There is a bus stop here if you prefer to miss out on downtown Arolla.) Continue straight ahead along the road/track past parking and after 15min, come to a **bridge** (1985m). Turn left across the bridge.

Climb steadily along a track, but after 4min, find a turn left heading (unfortunately, but only for 40m) downhill. Descend briefly through woods and onto pasture with views across to Arolla, with which you are now level. Climb again and come to a clearing with a large boulder with memorial plaques attached (30min from the start), one of which refers to Lhotse 1981.

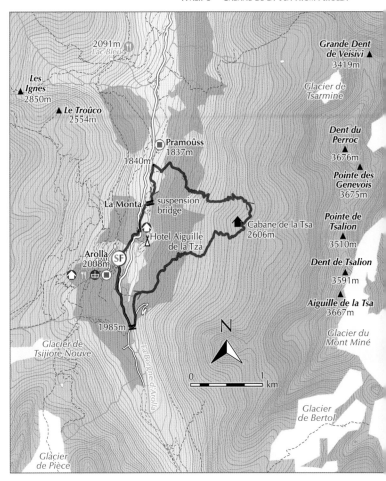

Continue to climb, at first steeply on a rocky path through woods and then at a slightly more relaxed angle as the trees reduce in size, with expanding views straight up to the Aiguille de la Tsa, but not the hut, which stays hidden until you are very nearly there. The path continually zigzags through rocky ground; the

The Pigne d'Arolla, Col de la Serpentine and Mont Blanc de Cheilon across the valley on the Tsa route

angle is reasonable and the walking without problems. As the hillside gets rockier, the hut comes into view on your left. Arrive at the **Cabane de la Tsa** (2606m, 2hr).

The **Cabane de la Tsa** is the start point for the many long rock climbs on the ridge above, including the Grande Dent de Veisivi, the Dent de Perroc and the unmissable spike of the Aiguille (needle) de la Tsa. The hut is owned by the local guides and accommodates 30. Refreshments are available.

Returning by the ascent route to Arolla takes about 1hr 30min, whereas the route described will take 2hr.

Continue past the hut, following a red sign to Pramoûss. Cross a well-laid-out route across a substantial boulder field for about 400m before the path starts determinedly downhill with large zigzags on the other side of the shallow valley

from the refuge. It steepens in places but generally keeps a good gradient. Enter trees at around 2200m and continue down. Soon the river is seen below through the trees. Pass by an electricity pylon and then follow a sign right to join a path by the river at **1840m** (3hr 20min). If heading straight down valley, the bus stop at Pramoûss is about 10min to the right.

For Arolla, turn left along the river, going gradually uphill. The path is directed away from the river. Come to a fine suspension bridge (the Passerelle de La Monta, around 65m across) and cross it, then turn left to pass through the hamlet of **La Monta**. Continue to the **Hotel Aiguille de la Tza**.

Double back briefly and cross the road to find a grassy track heading steadily uphill for the final 100m climb to Arolla in 20min. Pass under the terrace of the Hotel du Glacier to the road into **Arolla** (2008m, 4hr).

WALK 9
Arolla to Les Haudères – the valley route

Start	Arolla Poste (2008m)
Finish	Les Haudères bus stop (1451m)
Distance	9.5km
Total ascent	100m
Total descent	660m
Grade	1–2
Time	2hr 15min
Max altitude	2008m at Arolla
Refreshments	Arolla, La Gouille, Les Haudères
Access	Bus to Arolla

Almost entirely downhill, this beautiful route can be enjoyed by most walkers. Full of variety, the initial path from the village of Arolla drops steeply to pastures in the upper valley then crosses the river on a suspension bridge. The path then stays close to the braided river, recrossing it to visit the tiny hamlets of Satarma and La Gouille. From here onwards the route enters a narrow gorge, following a good track all the way to Les Haudères. Views are tremendous for the entire route.

The TVH follows this route as far as Les Haudères. A continuation to Evolène along the TVH is also outlined below.

From the bus turning area in the centre of Arolla by the Poste, head through the village on Rue de l'Évêque and take the descending path immediately to the right of the Hotel du Glacier. The path makes a couple of turns then descends through woods to emerge by the **Hotel Aiguille de la Tza**.

Cross the road and continue on the signed path ahead, across fields and between a cluster of chalets and barns (La Monta), then cross the suspension bridge. The path now drops almost level with the braided river. Just before reaching Satarma, turn left over a bridge, walk down the road, then fork left into the hamlet of **Satarma** (1805m, 1hr).

Walk through the hamlet, cross the main road and head over a bridge on a track through meadows, then recross the river and climb steeply up to the road

Palanche de
la Cretta
2929m

Forêt
du Dévin

Forêt des
Sanières

La Forclaz

N

0   1
km

Les Haudères
1451m

F

La Borgne d'Arolla

La Borgne de Ferpècle

St-Barthélémy
1823m

Petite Dent
de Veisivi
3184m

La Gouille
1835m

Grande Dent
de Veisivi
3419m

2091m
Lac Bleu

Glacier de
Tsarmine

Satarma
1805m

Le Troûco
2554m

Dent du
Perroc
3676m

Pramoûss
1837m

Pointe des
Genevois
3675m

La Monta

suspension
bridge

Cabane de la Tsa
2606m

Pointe de
Tsalion
3510m

Hotel Aiguille
de la Tza

Dent de Tsalion
3591m

Arolla
2008m

S

Aiguille de la Tsa
3667m

Traditional wooden buildings in Satarma

again. Turn right then fork left into the hamlet of **La Gouille** (1835m, 1hr 15min, refreshments).

La Gouille occupies a slightly elevated area at the point where the Borgne d'Arolla plunges steeply into a gorge, and it is at the base of a path to Lac Bleu, a popular beauty spot about 45min climb above the village (see Walk 6).

Return to the road, passing a tranquil tarn on the left, and after 50m take the descending path on the right just after a left bend. Keep to the left when the path forks, rising almost to the road, then descending to the tiny chapel of **St-Barthélémy**, nestled under a huge boulder. Now on a gravel track, continue ahead. When the track takes a sharp right turn, continue ahead, very steeply for a short while, then as the gradient lessens, enjoy the emerging views. The villages of La Forclaz, La Sage and Villa are perched above Les Haudères, which is directly ahead in the valley.

On reaching the main road just before Les Haudères, turn right and walk along it for 300m. Cross the Borgne de Ferpècle, then take the second turn on the right, passing to the right of the Hotel des Haudères, to arrive at the bus stop in the centre of **Les Haudères** (1451m, 2hr 15min).

Possible onward routes from Les Haudères to Evolène and La Sage
- To walk directly to Evolène, descend to cross over the river Borgne and follow the riverside path and track (reversing the route described in Walk 14) directly down the valley to reach **Evolène** (1hr 15min).

Looking down towards Les Haudères, the village of La Forclaz is seen on the shelf above

- For the continuing official TVH route via Evolène, pass above the Hotel des Haudères, then follow 'Walk 14 – Tour of the rock villages' from Les Haudères via La Forclaz to reach La Sage, passing the Hotel de la Sage. The chapel of St-Christophe is perched on a small hill just to the left. Continue up into the tiny village of **La Sage** (1668m, 1hr 30min).
- To avoid the descent to Evolène, and to pick up the continuing TVH route (Walk 21) directly at Villa, continue up the road through La Sage to reach Villa after a further 20min. A path contours the hillside to meet with the route out from Evolène.
- To continue down to Evolène, head back down past the Hotel de la Sage, turn right onto the 'Sentier Contemplatif', then join the route described in Walk 14 to reach the centre of **Evolène** (1372m, 1hr 45min).

WALK 10

Arolla to Evolène – the high Route 6

Start	Arolla Poste (2008m)
Finish	Evolène (1372m)
Distance	15km
Total ascent	860m
Total descent	1500m
Grade	3
Time	5hr 30min
Max altitude	2294m on the La Coûta hillside
Refreshments	Buvette at Lac Bleu, then none until Evolène
Access	Bus to Arolla

The high-level walking route from Arolla to Evolène is a gem of the region. It takes the so-called 'chemin difficile' route to the beautiful Lac Bleu and then makes a traverse through woods before climbing to a high pasture under Mont de l'Etoile. The route then gradually descends towards the valley, passing high farms and the attractive hamlet of L'Ata Gieute before dropping down on a pine-covered path to the charming village of Evolène. This walk follows Swiss Route 6 – the Alpine Passes trail – which crosses southern Switzerland, although signage for Route 6 is minimal between Arolla and Evolène.

For those on the TVH wanting to avoid the valley and villages of Stage 3, this makes a good alternative route. It may be even better in reverse, walking towards the high mountains, but it is a long climb out of Evolène so allow 6hr 30min.

From Arolla Poste take the Rue de l'Évêque away from the village's centre hairpin. After 40m turn left, up steps, opposite the Hotel du Glacier, then continue past buildings. After 12min pass a turn right for the easier route to Lac Bleu (described in Walk 6). Turn left up the path signed 'chemin difficile', which immediately becomes rockier. The 'difficile' is arguably exaggerated so don't be deterred – its label is designed to put off the inexperienced – but it does have a section of Grade 3 path traversing steep ground high above the valley.

The first half of the 'chemin difficile' trends uphill and the second half downhill, but there is nearly 350m of up and 250m of down between Arolla and Lac Bleu, so it is undulating all the way. Come to the first chain section after 35min; there are five sections, all short, and the chains are perhaps more reassuring than necessary. Cross two bridges over a stream after 1hr 5min and join with the lower path after 1hr 15min. Cross another stream and then climb before arriving at **Lac Bleu** (2091m, 1hr 30min).

> **Lac Bleu** is a popular place to visit so you are very unlikely to have it to yourself. From some angles the lake is decidedly green, but it is without doubt one of the most beautiful lakes in the Alps. There is a small buvette 2min below the outflow, along the route. If you need to leave the route, this is one of the few opportunities and the descent to La Gouille takes about 30min.

Continue on the Evolène path above the buvette, through attractive woods before reaching a more open hillside. After 2hr, another path from La Gouille merges with our route, which continues traversing and undulating, alternating between woods and open mountainside. The path starts to rise in earnest to a large cross and a small shepherd's building protected from above by a large rock.

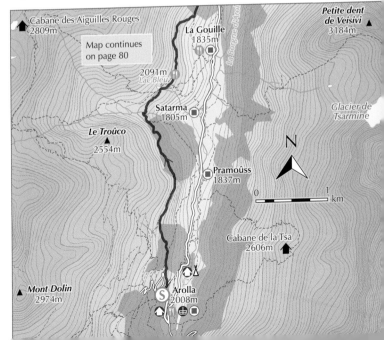

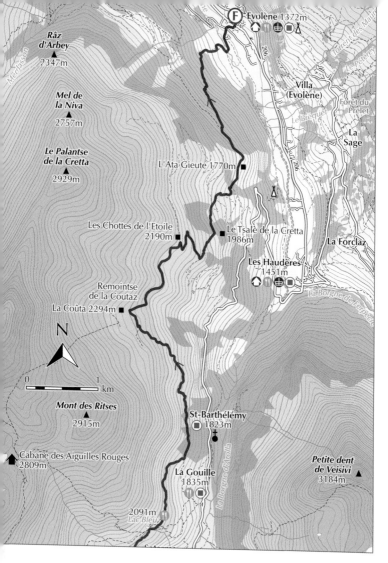

This marks the halfway point (7.5km), at about 2294m on the **La Coûta** hillside, and is reached after 3hr.

Continue, crossing a stream where there may be risk of stonefall below the Remointse de la Coutaz. Traverse a smaller and then a larger mountain bowl and arrive at the modernised farm at **Les Chottes de l'Etoile** (2190m, 3hr 35min). Views across the Ferpècle valley and of the Dent Blanche are exceptional from here, as is the view back to Arolla and Mont Collon.

Descend on the farm track for 15min and turn left at a junction at 2092m. Pass above the largely abandoned hamlet of Le Tsalè de la Cretta, and then continue into woods before coming to the houses around Les Mayens de la Cretta. The path crosses a service track three times, so keep a look out for the yellow signs. At 1768m the path firmly joins with the good track that heads north to the hamlet of **L'Ata Gieute** (1770m).

Continue past the hamlet on the tarmacked track that soon becomes a grassy trail reminiscent of a route from another century. Ten minutes after the hamlet find a right turn signed to Evolène, which can be clearly seen through gaps in the trees.

The first half of the final descent is on a comfortable bed of pine needles, and the bottom half gets steeper as it drops into pastures facing the village across the river. Pass farm buildings and come to the bridge over the Borgne river. Turn left and come to a road junction. Go straight ahead, curving right before a final pull up to the centre of **Evolène** (1372m, 5hr 30min).

The hamlet of L'Ata Gieute is a surprise before the descent into Evolène, with La Sage and Villa across the valley

LES HAUDÈRES AND FERPÈCLE

WALK 11

Roc Vieux from Les Haudères

Start/finish	Les Haudères (1451m)
Alternative start	Bus stop at Les Jutes (1823m) (St-Barthélémy)
Distance	12km (10km)
Total ascent	950m (630m)
Total descent	950m (1000m)
Grade	2
Time	5hr (4hr from Les Jutes)
Max altitude	2286m
Refreshments	None on route
Access	Bus to Les Haudères and/or Les Jutes

Roc Vieux dominates the junction between the Ferpècle and Arolla valleys, looming high over Les Haudères with the twin peaks of the Dents du Veisivi above. It's a fine viewpoint, stretching from the Dent Blanche at the head of the Ferpècle valley all the way round to the peaks and glaciers of Mont Blanc de Cheilon.

This walk is described as an out-and-back route from Les Haudères; however, an alternative start from the bus stop at Les Jutes (one stop before La Gouille) saves over 300m of ascent and 1hr of walking time.

Note that Roc Vieux is named on all the signs but not the Swisstopo maps.

From the centre of Les Haudères take the main road across the bridge over the Borgne de Ferpècle in the direction of Arolla, then immediately after crossing the Borgne d'Arolla bridge, turn left up a metalled road (Route de Pralovin). This soon becomes a gravel track once you have passed the houses, and climbs through two hairpins. Continue up the track climbing steadily. Once the ancient route to Arolla, this track leads all the way to a junction of tracks at **1744m** (1hr 15min).

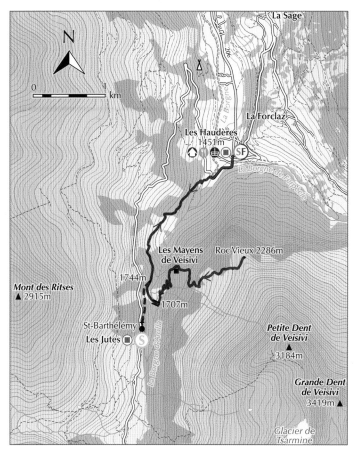

This is where the track down from the bus stop in Les Jutes meets the track from Les Haudères.

Alternative start from Les Jutes
Find the path opposite the bus stop and turn left, descending steadily past the tiny chapel of **St-Barthélémy**, nestled under a huge boulder, to reach the 1744m track junction (saves 1hr walking time).

The Pigne d'Arolla and Mont Blanc de Cheilon seen from just below Roc Vieux

Main route

Take the descending track signed for Roc Vieux, cross the bridge over the Borgne d'Arolla, then climb the track in big loops at a steady gradient to arrive at the cluster of chalets and barns at **Les Mayens de Veisivi** (1877m, 1hr 40min). These are referred to as 'Lu Veijuvi' on some maps.

Pass in front of the two higher buildings, then follow the path around just below the small hillock and continue to climb steadily, heading to the right just below the edge of the trees. Now the steep ascent begins! Climb steeply up to a small gate, with a large, rocky ravine just to the right. Once through the gate, the path leads all the way to Roc Vieux. Much of the walk is through beautiful larch woods, always steep, but the path is well made and there is no difficulty. After about 20min through the woods, arrive at a slightly flatter pasture area; sheep may be grazing here. Follow red-and-white paint splashes on the

scattered boulders and continue up through more woodland. The final 80m of ascent is over open hillside covered in bilberry bushes, with superb views south towards Mont Blanc de Cheilon. Finally, reach a cross and signpost indicating **Roc Vieux** (2286m, 3hr).

The views are superb in almost every direction, the distant **Dent Blanche** dominating the view up the Ferpècle valley to the east. There is a real sense of space and height here. The cliff drops off abruptly just beyond the cross, so take care!

To go down, reverse the route taken on the ascent. Buses from Les Jutes are infrequent, so it will almost certainly be best to return to **Les Haudères** by walking down the track.

WALK 12
Ferpècle valley

Start/finish	Les Haudères village centre bus stop (1451m)
Distance	16km
Total ascent	660m
Total descent	660m
Grade	2
Time	5hr
Max altitude	2000m on high path above dam
Refreshments	Le Petit Paradis, La Forclaz (200m off-route), Les Haudères
Access	Daily bus from Les Haudères in July and August; weekends only at other times during the season

Exploring the Ferpècle valley is a treat to be saved for a good, clear day. As you walk along the path on the north side of the valley, the views up to the Dents de Veisivi on the opposite side of the valley grow with every step. Glaciers tumble down from the Dent Blanche, which dominates the scene, while Mont Miné casts a dark silhouette between the Ferpècle and Mont Miné glaciers. The upper valley is a truly spectacular place: wild and beautiful.

From the bus stop, pass above the Hotel des Haudères and turn right up between the houses, then turn right again and then left onto the road to La Forclaz. After 100m fork off to the right just before the first hairpin bend, then take the signed path left below a chalet, with a works area below. The path is predominantly uphill, passing tremendous rock formations as you gain height.

> The **rocks** beside the path have been eroded by glacial and subglacial streams, giving a smooth almost swirling profile, with overhanging areas much appreciated by rock climbers.

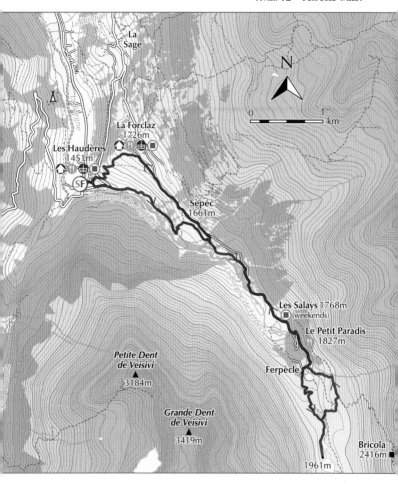

On reaching an open meadow, take the rising path left to reach the hamlet of **Sepéc** (1661m, 50min). This little cluster of houses is typical of the area, with alp pastures surrounding the settlement.

With much of the steeper climbing now behind you, enjoy the track across the meadows, and after 10min take the path to the right on a left-hand bend in

Easy walking up the Ferpècle valley towards the Dent Blanche

the track and cross a stream. Cross another stream shortly after, then continue on the path as it rises to reach the valley road. Turn right and walk up the road. It's generally very quiet, with little traffic. Pass the bus stop at **Les Salays**, with the now closed Hotel du Col d'Hérens, and continue for a further 20min to reach **Le Petit Paradis** (1827m, 2hr, refreshments).

Continue on the road, passing a sign on the left for a path, then turn up the gravel track to the left. There is ample parking to the right, for those who have missed the walk so far! Follow the gravel track as it climbs past a dam in lazy loops through a protected alluvial area, with tremendous views ahead of glaciers and peaks and the infant Borgne de Ferpècle swirling a little below. Pass a signed path to the left next to an information board and continue beside the river as far as you wish, although the path beyond the small lake at point **1961m** becomes less distinct.

UPPER FÈRPECLE VALLEY

The views at this point are sublime. Above to the left is the Dent Blanche (4357m), draped with glaciers from below the Arête de Ferpècle. To the right is the dark silhouette of Mont Miné, with the Mont Miné icefall tumbling over a rock buttress on its right. The glaciers have receded considerably over the last 50 years, as the bare rock testifies. Braided streams flow across the outwash area before being captured for power generation further downstream. The Bricola building (2416m) can be seen perched high on a shelf below the Dent Blanche (see Walk 13).

Leaving this scene, retrace the route as far as the information board, then turn right and cross the stream. The path heads left at first then bends right just before reaching a small barn and climbs steadily to reach another barn. Turn left immediately behind this and continue to climb. As you look back, the Mont Miné icefall is truly spectacular.

At a path junction, either turn sharp left, descending directly to the dam, or, for better views, continue up to the next path junction and turn left onto a smaller level path at 2000m. After 300m turn left just before a deep ravine and descend the lightly wooded hillside to the road.

Retrace the route along the road for just under 2km, then turn left onto the path just before a road tunnel. Follow the path for 1km, then just after the second stream crossing turn right onto the track to join the road again. The road passes above the hamlet of **Sepéc** then levels around the hillside, enjoying extensive views, to arrive at a road junction on the outskirts of the village of **La Forclaz** (1726m, 4hr 30min). For refreshments, walk up the main road for 150m to find a hotel.

> **La Forclaz** is one of the rock villages perched high above the main Val d'Hérens. These are mainly traditional villages, where ancient chalets and barns predominate. La Sage and Villa share the same alp landscape above steep rock cliffs, all at around 1700m, and can be visited in turn on Walk 15.

Take the left fork, descending towards the old part of the village, then turn left onto a gravel track just before the village centre. Follow the track down across broad hay meadows dotted with chalets and barns, then turn right onto a path near the final chalet, descending more steeply to arrive back in **Les Haudères** (1451m, 5hr).

The Dent Blanche and Mont Miné dominate above the glacial outwash area. The Bricola building is visible on the ridge to the left

WALK 13
Bricola and the upper Ferpècle valley

Start/finish	Ferpècle bus stop at Les Salays (1768m)
Distance	11km
Total ascent	660m
Total descent	660m
Grade	2
Time	4hr 20min
Max altitude	2416m at Bricola
Refreshments	Le Petit Paradis, below the dam
Access	Daily bus from Les Haudères in July and August; weekends only at other times during the season

To fully appreciate the incredible landscape and skyline of the upper regions of the Ferpècle valley, and for the best views of the mighty Dent Blanche, this is the walk to tackle. In high summer a bus service operates as far as Les Salays (weekends only at other times), but many take a car to park in one of the parking areas a little higher.

Once you're off the road, a good path leads through woods and open mountainside all the way. The path is often shared with mountaineers making their way up to a high hut ready to tackle an ascent of the Dent Blanche, a further 2000m above Bricola.

From the bus stop walk up the road and continue through two hairpin bends (a small, rough path cuts across a bend) to pass **Le Petit Paradis** restaurant (20min), then continue up the road for a further 5min to find a path signed to Bricola on the left.

At first through woods then an open grassy hillside, the path rises steadily for about 1km then swings more uphill to the left. Ignore the path joining from the right and at a junction of paths next to a water trough, turn right. This almost level path leads to another path junction in 150m, where you turn left, signed for the Bivouac Dent Blanche and Bricola (1hr).

Climb steadily and fairly steeply in broad zigzags at first, then continue on the path as it threads through and above rocky outcrops in tight bends. A slightly

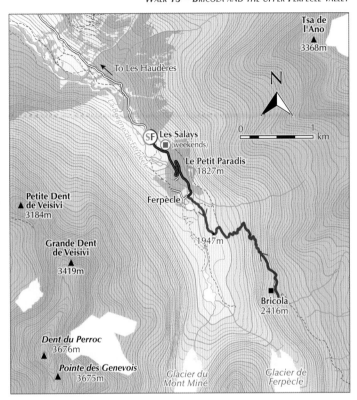

awkward collection of boulders leads to a stream crossing in a gully with a short cabled section for reassurance. Take the right fork in the path (the left fork is a little exposed in places) and soon arrive at **Bricola** (2416m, 2hr 30min).

> It is possible to climb above **Bricola**, but the going quickly becomes rough and steep. It's a glaciated climb to the Cabane de la Dent Blanche at 3507m, described on the SAC website as an 'important and painful elevation'.

After enjoying the scene for as long as you wish, return down into the valley by the same path. Allow approximately 1hr 30min for the return walk to the bus stop.

The Bricola building, Mont Miné to the left and the lower slopes of the Dent du Perroc to the right

BRICOLA VIEWPOINT

The four-story building, once a refuge, is currently owned by the Grande Dixence scheme. The best views are just beyond the building, past the semi-ruined barns. Ahead the Dent Blanche (4357m) looms 2000m above, draped with glaciers, the most spectacular being the Ferpècle glacier, which flows from the Plateau d'Hérens ice sheet. The deep valley carved by this glacier drops over 300m below. To the right, the Mont Miné glacier tumbles over a rock shelf in a jumbled icefall, with Mont Miné (2913m) separating the two.

EVOLÈNE

WALK 14

Tour of the rock villages – Route 214

Start/finish	Evolène village centre (1372m)
Distance	12km (7.5km if starting in Les Haudères)
Total ascent	570m
Total descent	570m
Grade	1–2
Time	4hr (or 2hr 45min if starting in Les Haudères)
Max altitude	1730m at the col above La Forclaz
Refreshments	Les Haudères, La Forclaz, La Sage and Villa
Access	Bus services to all villages

This fine walk explores the villages high above the cliffs of Evolène and Les Haudères, following waymarked Route 214 (Tour of the rock villages) for most of the way.

With your back to the church in Evolène village centre, walk down the paved path between chalets, crossing a road onto a track down to the river. Noticeboards provide information about the Lotrey (Lotrec) Alluvial Protected Area. Cross the bridge and turn left on the track across meadows dotted with isolated hay barns. Fork right at the next bridge and climb easily to about 1430m, then descend through woods to the riverside, with the Nordic Arena seen just across the river (used for cow-fighting contests in the summer, Nordic sporting events in winter and other valley events). Turn right beside the river, then left over the bridge and follow yellow footpath markers into the village of **Les Haudères** (1451m, 1hr 15min).

The pretty village of Les Haudères

LES HAUDÈRES

Occupying a strategic location at the junction of the Ferpècle and Arolla valleys, Les Haudères lies at the foot of the twin peaks of the Points de Veisivi. The heart of the old village of Les Haudères is on the east side of the main road. A little roadside chapel dated 1925 is decorated with painted murals. Many of the houses in the old part of the village are several hundred years old, interspersed with barns set on staddle stones to prevent rodents from entering. The houses are several stories high, designed to maximise the available land for grazing and farming, and each story once would have housed an entire family. A geology and glaciology museum can be found opposite the Hotel Dents de Veisivi.

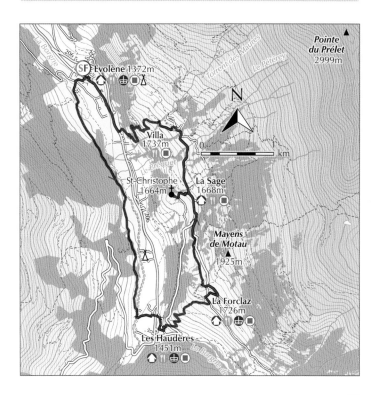

Walk through the main street and follow signs for La Sage, then after 150m take a rising path sharply to the right at Les Foches. Cross the road and climb the path then track to meet the village road. Turn left and follow signs up through the village of **La Forclaz** (1726m, 2hr).

LA FORCLAZ

La Forclaz has fine views up the Ferpècle valley to the Dent Blanche and towards Arolla, with Mont Blanc de Cheilon visible in the far distance. The community is centred on farming, and old barns and chalets are intermingled with more modern developments. A few shops and a hotel are located on the main road above.

Just after the village square area fork right, rising to meet the main road next to a hotel (refreshments). Turn left and walk up the road to the bus stop by a small car park. Take the small descending track in the far right-hand corner of the small parking area, then turn right after about 50m and follow this track across meadows. Pass a sign (left) for Evolène, then fork left below a large building, with the road seen just above. The grassy track shortly meets the road, which descends to a hairpin bend. Continue straight ahead on a quieter road rising to pass Restaurant L'Ecureuil, in **La Sage** (1668m, 2hr 45min).

LA SAGE

La Sage also enjoys commanding views in all directions, especially from the little chapel of St-Christophe, seen on the hillock to the left. The village is often used as an overnight stage for walking the Tour du Val d'Hérens, and by Chamonix–Zermatt trekkers before tackling either the Col du Tsaté or Col de Torrent.

To visit the chapel, fork left immediately after passing the restaurant and descend in a zigzag past the Hotel de la Sage (refreshments), then fork left. Turn right onto the signed path up to the chapel just after a line of chalets. Note that the chapel may be locked.

From the chapel, return towards the Hotel de la Sage, and note a sign for Route 214, part of the 'Sentier Contemplatif', onto a path ahead just below the hotel. This joins the path from Villa but misses out the village of Villa (also spelt Villaz or Villars). To visit Villa, return to the road just above the hotel and turn left onto Route des Rocs. The road isn't busy and you soon arrive at **Villa** (1737m, 3hr 30min, refreshments).

VILLA

The little chapel is simply decorated and open for visitors. Restaurant Col de Torrent is located at the end of the road by the bus stop.

Take the path signed to the left down narrow stone steps at the side of the chapel and continue down on a well-made path between chalets and barns. The path becomes a gravel track threading between meadows then sweeping left to join the Route 214 track coming directly from La Sage at L'Omâzo. Turn right and begin a steeper descent on a good path through woods, with glimpses of the near-vertical cliffs above Evolène, seen far below. Follow this path all the way down to reach the road, turn right and walk back into **Evolène** (1372m, 4hr).

EVOLÈNE

Evolène is the principal village in the upper regions of the Val d'Hérens. This thriving community provides good facilities, including a range of shops, hotels and restaurants, and accommodation options, including a campsite. The old central area of the village is well preserved, and many of the stone and wooden buildings have been sympathetically renovated, retaining original features externally.

The chapel of St Christophe above La Sage, with the village of Villa behind

WALK 15

Evolène to Pralong (Dix valley) via Col de la Meina

Start	Evolène (1372m)
Finish	Pralong (1608m)
Distance	15.5km
Total ascent	1410m
Total descent	1180m
Grade	3
Time	6hr 30min
Max altitude	2702m on the Col de la Meina
Refreshments	None on the route, until Pralong; Arbey, 20min off-route after the first hour
Access	Bus to Evolène and bus from Pralong, change at Vex to return to Evolène

The walk follows the route of an ancient pass between Evolène and the Val des Dix. It's an up-and-down affair, 1400m up then nearly 1200m down. With fine views to the east as you approach the col, the Dent Blanche and the Weisshorn only add to the spectacle. On the descent there are views to the Dix dam and mountains beyond. The descent is also a matter of two halves; at first rugged over rocky slopes, after a midway alpage it follows an old mule track that descends comfortably to the hamlet of Pralong and a welcoming café/restaurant.

The route can be done in reverse. Allow 3hr 30min for the climb, with a slow finish on the rockier upper section. The descent to Evolène is long, but there is the possibility of diverting to the Lanna chairlift, saving 30–60min (see Walk 17), or refreshments at Arbey.

From the centre of Evolène head downhill, following Route 6, then turn right at the road and follow it across the river and round the first hairpin to find a sign and path heading uphill (10min).

Turn left and start the climb on a forest path that has been in use for centuries. Pass a left turn to Arbey after 20min but keep straight on unless you intend to

Passing the bowl of the Glacier de Vouasson, cradled by Mont de l'Etoile, and the Pointe de Vouasson on the climb to the Col de la Meina

divert there for early refreshments. Cross a track and then a road but keep straight ahead, coming to a junction at **1680m** after 1hr 5min, where you turn right.

Continue on the climb, which veers into and then crosses the deep indentation of the Merdechon stream. Soon after, arrive at the buildings of **Le Vernec** (1881m, 1hr 45min). Keep climbing and soon leave the sheltering woods behind and pass the **Tsalè de la Vouasson**, a largely abandoned series of alp farm buildings. Pass under a small ski tow three times and join a track to come to the **Pas d'Arpilles** (2435m, 3hr 15min). It's not a pass, more a gate, but it opens the way to higher views from Vouasson to the col.

Head into the high grazing, which, initially, is a more gradual climb. Keep an eye open for patous guarding the flocks that graze here. Go round the flocks, but if the dogs decide to inspect you, stay calm as they confirm you don't represent a threat to the sheep. Turn left at a junction and left again at a junction at **2627m**. If you decide to climb Pic d'Artsinol (2997m), turn right here (1hr up and 40min down – see Walk 17). To continue, turn left at the junction and climb to the **Col de la Meina** (2702m, 4hr 10min).

From the col, take the downward path, which crosses boulders, climbs and drops across the immense mountainside. At first, head left then switch right, climbing and dropping through the boulders. After 300m the hillside gets grassier. At 50min from the col you will pass the small buildings at the **Remointse de Novèlé** (2402m, 5hr).

Continue down on a steadily improving path with innumerable zigzags to the tumbledown alpage buildings at **Novèlé** (2082m, 5hr 30min).

Pass above the buildings and just after them find the sign; left heads to the Barrage de la Grande Dixance in about 1hr 45min, so keep to the right-hand path that descends. Suddenly all is different. The path, an ancient track designed for mules, drops steadily, with pine needles to comfort the feet. Pass a building at 1810m but continue on the path. At one point as the path enters a clearing, it seems to disappear. Keep right here and find a gate for the continuation. At

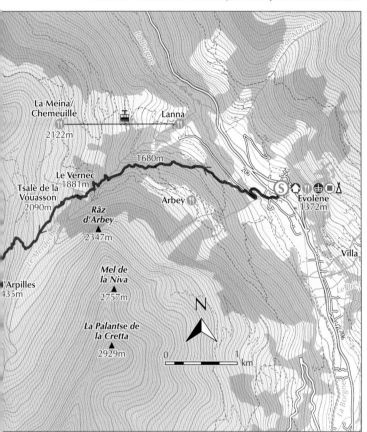

1670m, pass above the chalets of **Les Tsepès** to find the continuing path that joins a road and soon arrives in **Pralong** (1608m, 6hr 30min).

> **Pralong** is a tiny settlement in the Val d'Hérémence, with a hotel/restaurant and campsite, as well as a bus stop for the return to the start. Return to Evolène by bus, changing at Vex.

WALK 16
Pic d'Artsinol

Start/finish	La Meina/Chemeuille at the top of the Lanna ski lift (2122m)
Distance	11km
Total ascent	900m (875m on the ascent)
Total descent	900m
Grade	2–3
Time	4hr 30min (2hr 20min on the ascent)
Max altitude	2997m at the summit of Pic d'Artsinol
Refreshments	None on the route, only at the La Meina/Chemeuille lift station at the start/end of the route
Access	Walk (30min) or drive to Lanna and lift to Chemeuille (20min) (ie, allow about 1hr from Evolène to La Meina if walking)

Pic d'Artsinol must be one of the finest viewpoints in the western Alps. Standing alone on a ridge above Evolène, it has 360-degree views encompassing Mont Blanc, the Matterhorn and the Jungfrau, as well as nearer peaks, with the Dent Blanche dominating the eastern side of the Hérens valley. The initial climb is on a track, and the steeper upper section on good paths with almost no exposure. Make sure you have a good weather day to enjoy the best views.

From the top of the lift, head slightly downhill past the restaurant and turn sharply left. Pass the Chemeuille farm. Cheese and butter can be bought here but best buy them on the way down – it's a long way up first. Keep on the track, looking ahead into the still-glaciated bowl under Pointe de Vouasson and Mont de l'Etoile. After 30min, and still on the track, take a sharp right hairpin turn at **2262m**. The descending track rejoins here later in the day.

Ten minutes later, as you approach the high farm at **La Noûva**, keep left as the track swings round. The track steepens and comes out by a small hut and path junction under a ski tow at **2577m** (1hr 15min). Take the path right, signed to the peak. Pass the top of the ski tow and make a left turn around a rock outcrop,

where the path levels at a 2678m path junction. From here to the ridge is a steep climb, but eventually you will come out at a low point on the ridge at **2801m** (1hr 50min).

The climb to the summit is on a broad ridge, so head steadily upwards. It is less steep than the climb to the ridge. Cross a rocky section, then the well-worn path leads the way to the summit of **Pic d'Artsinol** (2997m, 2hr 20min).

Allow plenty of time on the summit to explore the **360-degree views**. To the west the Dents du Midi are prominent, then the Mont Blanc range and

Summit cross and sculpture on Pic d'Artsinol

Mont Blanc itself, then the Combin range. Closer is the Dix dam and the peaks around it, Mont Blanc de Cheilon (milk pail) and La Rosablanche, and the outlines of the peaks above Verbier can be seen further to the west.

To the north the Wildhorn and Wildstrubel ranges are seen, with their small glaciers to identify them. The peaks above Kandersteg and the Bernese Oberland are prominent, the snow-covered Jungfrau clearly visible. To the east lie the Weisshorn, Zinalrothorn and Dent Blanche, with the Matterhorn looking unusually small behind the Dent Blanche.

Once you have digested the fabulous view, it is time to head down, initially to the 2801m ridge turn (not waymarked so take care to spot it after about 25min), then the steep descent to the 2678m junction. Keep right here, currently the sign is damaged. If you return by the ascent route by keeping left, you will save 30min overall.

The path drops gradually, and after 10min you will arrive at another path junction, at 2627m.

> From here it is straightforward to climb the **Col de la Meina**, a walkers' pass between the Val d'Hérens and the Val d'Hérémence with views over the Dixence barrage (described in Walk 15). Allow 30min for the 1.25km, 80m climb and descent.

As well as the climb to the col, there are other options at the 2627m path junction. Turn left, then after dropping about 30m either turn left to rejoin the ascent route by the 2577m hut and the track back, or, for the more varied route described here, turn right.

Drop down gradually through a large grassy bowl. If there are sheep here, they may well be attended by patou dogs (see Introduction). If you prefer to avoid them, turn left at the junction rather than right. The path levels out to come to a gate, signed the **Pas d'Arpilles** at 2435m.

Go through the gate and continue the descent. After 5min the path dropping directly to Evolène heads right, off the track, but keep left here, staying on the

Looking south-east from the summit, with the Weisshorn, Zinalrothorn and Dent Blanche

track. It soon becomes a narrow path traversing the hill and emerges at the **2262m** path junction passed on the ascent (4hr).

From here take the track down to **Chemeuille** (4hr 30min). Buy cheese if needed and certainly enjoy the bar and restaurant before taking the lift down to **Lanna** to return to Evolène.

WALK 17

Evolène to Pralong (Dix valley) via Mandelon

Start	Top of chairlift from Lanna (above Evolène) to La Meina (2122m)
Finish	Pralong (1608m)
Distance	12km
Total ascent	250m
Total descent	760m
Grade	2
Time	3hr 40min
Max altitude	2250m at Montagne de Vendes
Refreshments	Restaurants at La Meina, Mandelon Alpage (2069m) and at Pralong
Access	Chairlift from Lanna to La Meina; bus stops at Léteygeon and Pralong to Vex (with connection to Val d'Hérens). Vehicle access and parking at Mandelon Alpage. The walk from Evolène to Lanna takes 30min

For those looking for a relatively easy walk with superb views, possible opportunities to see chamois and several good restaurant options, this is a walk to put near the top of the list. The linear route described uses public transport, or it's possible to walk out and back between Mandelon Alpage and La Meina in 4hr 30min, saving about 500m of downhill.

The route undulates generally uphill from La Meina (Chemeuille), with good views across the valley towards Becs de Bosson, down into the Rhône valley and beyond, and up to the craggy summit of Pic d'Artsinol. Entering the Dixence valley, the route passes the Mandelon Alpage, with views towards the huge Dixence barrage and across to the mountain ranges to the west between Dix and Verbier.

From the top of the chairlift at Chemeuille, take the track north, just above the restaurant, then after 2min fork left on a slightly rougher track. Climb steadily to reach a height of around 2200m and continue, now on a path, around the hillside, with a huge bowl up to the left and the pinnacles and towers of Pic d'Artsinol, Mont

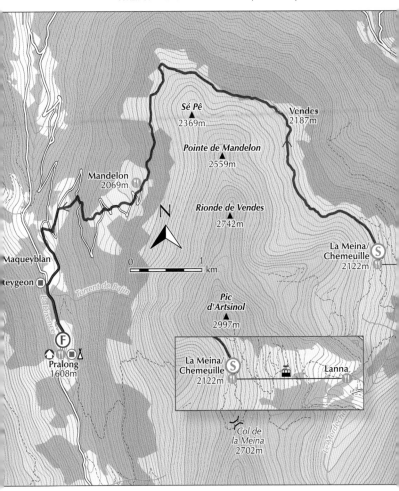

Rouge and Rionde de Vendes creating a dramatic skyline. Undulating around this height, the path crosses a hillside covered with bilberry, alpenrose and juniper, and views stretch in all directions. You will reach a signpost to Euseigne above the alp hamlet of **Vendes** (2187m, 1hr).

Continue above the houses to reach a tiny tarn with tremendous views up into the mountains – Pointe de Mandelon and Sé Pê above. It's a lovely spot to linger. The route now has a more intimate feel for a while, being slightly less open, with flowers, shrubs and scattered trees and yet increasingly extensive views across to Vex and the villages scattered above. The path gradually widens to a track, reaching a high point at about 2250m (1hr 15min).

> This area of **grassy hillside** and light woodland is a haven for wildlife, and you may well spot chamois as they effortlessly negotiate the hillside. Cameras attached to trees are part of a widespread project monitoring the location and movement of larger predators – lynx, wolves and bears.

The track makes a sharp turn to the left in light pine woodland and suddenly the views ahead are to the south, up the length of the Dixence valley to the huge Grande Dixence barrage, and across to the long, ragged ridgeline to the west. The track descends gently, passing an isolated barn at Pramosson, then continues down to reach the **Mandelon Alpage and restaurant** (2069m, 2hr).

Walkers descend into the Val des Dix, towards Mandelon Alpage

Mandelon is a large dairy alp – a huge barn with a distinctive larch-shingle roof adjoining the restaurant, and a smaller chalet selling home-produced cheeses, jam and soap. It's a popular location, with seating inside and out enjoying panoramic views, and has ample parking.

Suitably refreshed, cross the car park then take the descending path by a cross over meadows as it crosses and recrosses the road between hairpins. At first the route is not signed, but the path is clearly marked on the map and is also clear on the ground. Enter forest on an ancient forest track to reach the road 45min from the alpage. From here on the route is well signed. Turn right then left down past a few houses to reach the road again. Turn left and walk down the road, then drop down to the right onto a signed path to meet the road by a tall mast. Turn right, then immediately after the houses seen below turn left and descend to meet the road yet again, with a picnic area and water.

Walk down the road for 1km to reach the main valley road and a bus stop at **Léteygeon** (3hr 20min). To continue up the valley to **Pralong** (1608m), with its restaurant and bar, walk up the road for a further 1km (3hr 40min).

WALK 18

Euseigne pyramids, Ossona, the passerelle and Combioule hot springs

Start/finish	Euseigne village bus stop (975m)
Distance	12km
Total ascent	610m
Total descent	610m
Grade	2
Time	4hr
Max altitude	1040m
Refreshments	Auberge d'Ossona
Access	Bus to Euseigne from up or down the valley

This walk has several highlights all rolled into one route. Shoes or boots with a good grip are essential as some sections are quite steep. The traverse below St Martin has occasional exposed sections leading to the 133m Grande Combe suspension bridge, which is very stable and fun to cross, soon leading to the Auberge d'Ossona (Ossone) for refreshments and great views. The descent to the riverbed and Combioule hot springs is steep, followed by close-up views of the Euseigne Pyramids at Euseigne.

From the village centre bus stop, walk down the paved road, away from the main road, and turn right onto Rue de Champclou, pass a general store and walk up to rejoin the main road. Cross over then turn left onto Chemin de Tejet. The road leads to a track then a path through woodland, keeping high above the road. Cross bridges over small gorges then descend to **La Luette** (35min).

Turn right and walk beside the road for 300m, then just after crossing the bridge into the village, take the ramp down to the left signed to 'Ossone'. The path descends steeply in zigzags to a bridge over the river, then climbs up to join a track, signed 'Ossone Route 215'. The rising track passes a small chalet on the left then turns left onto a grassy track at **1002m** (1hr). This level track leads past a small orchard and chalets at Les Abelires to end at a gate.

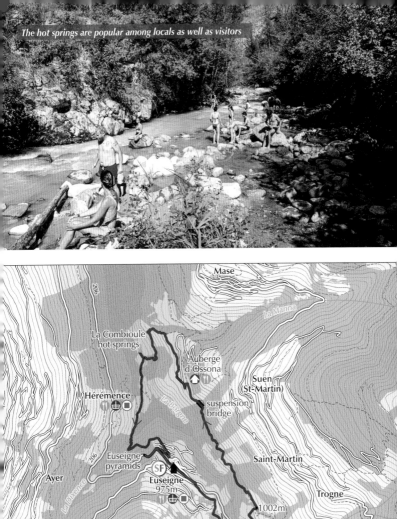

The hot springs are popular among locals as well as visitors

Les Abelires is part of an agritourism initiative to restore the habitat of the hillside in this area.

Take the descending path which zigzags then continues into woods, dropping for about 60m then undulating continuously as it traverses the moraine hillside. While much of this 2km section of the route is in woodland, there are occasional good views across the valley to the pyramids. The path is well maintained, but has a few sections where chains are provided for assistance, or reassurance, as you approach the **suspension bridge** (1hr 45min).

Cross with care, enjoying more great views, then continue on the path for a further 15min, descend to a track and turn right to arrive at the **Auberge d'Ossona** (2hr, refreshments, accommodation).

The hamlet of **Ossona** has been restored thanks to an agritourism initiative and now has the auberge, self-catering accommodation, a cheese cellar, a solar system and grazing for goats and cows on the near-level terraced hillside.

Walk up the signed path between chalets above the auberge then turn left at the signpost and follow an almost level path indicated with green and white posts. This leads around the left-hand side of a large flat pasture, where the goats graze happily, and you will come to a signpost and gate (2hr 15min).

Go through the gate and take the steep path down, firstly to a small, reno-vated house, then continue steeply, taking care as the surface is loose and stony. After a brief flatter section, descend again in tight turns to reach a bridge over the river in the valley floor. Cross over, turn right, then recross the river on another bridge and turn left. Follow this path through trees and bushes to arrive at the **Combioule hot springs**, with several small pools created next to the river (2hr 35min). If you've brought suitable dipping clothes, feel free to take a dip.

The **Borgne river** runs along a fault line. Warm water emerges at several points but the Combioule springs are the most well known. Rainwater seeps into the fractured rocks along the fault line at high altitude, then slowly descends over 800m underground where it is gradually warmed during the course of several decades, absorbing minerals and salts. Rapid travel to the surface prevents the water from cooling, resulting in hot springs of around 29 °C.

Retrace your steps to the bridge, then continue up the gravel track climbing to reach a metalled road at a hairpin. Walk up the road, then continue on a track ahead at a bend and descend slightly to cross the Dixence river. A shaded, grassy track climbs in zigzags, passing under the line of pyramids at a height of about

900m. Continue, to reach the first houses of Euseigne and walk up the metalled road to the second hairpin bend and turn sharply right. (At the time of writing the paths past Les Terrasses, and above the pyramids, were closed.)

The minor road leads up to the main road, with the pyramids seen directly ahead. There is generally little traffic, so walking along the road to the pyramids for photographs should be safe. Now retrace your route but continue beside the main road into the village of **Euseigne** (975m, 4hr).

EUSEIGNE PYRAMIDS

These incredible earth cones were formed towards the end of the last ice age, between 80,000 and 10,000 years ago. The cones are between 10m and 15m high, and since 1983 they have been listed and protected in Switzerland's Federal Inventory of Landscapes and Natural Monuments of National Importance. They are one of the most unique landscapes in the Alps.

Water erosion has carved out much of the moraine material, which in this case is resistant to dissolving. The boulders on the tops of the cones have acted as umbrellas, protecting some of the moraine from erosion, leaving these unique spires.

The Euseigne pyramids from just below Euseigne

WALK 19
Villa to Grimentz via Col de Torrent

Start	Villa (1737m)
Finish	Grimentz cable-car station (1590m)
Distance	17km
Total ascent	1200m
Total descent	1350m
Grade	2–3
Time	6hr 15min (3hr to the Col de Torrent)
Max altitude	2916m at the col
Refreshments	None above Villa; restaurant at the Moiry barrage
Access	Bus to Villa from Les Haudères. Buses in the Val d'Anniviers from Grimentz and cablecar to Zinal

The Col de Torrent is one of the gateway cols between the Val d'Hérens and the Val d'Anniviers. It's a well-graded path, classified as yellow until 2500m and remaining straightforward right to the col and down to Moiry. As part of the Haute Route, it leads to the Lac de Moiry and the 2826m Cabane de Moiry, as well as Grimentz and Zinal. For walkers headed west, it provides access to Evolène and the villages above. But the col is a good destination in its own right, a full 1200m above the hamlet of Villa. For those trained and equipped, it accesses peaks to the north and the south. Views on the way up include the entire Hérens valley, particularly the Dent Blanche, while from the col, the Weisshorn and other peaks above Zinal can be seen.

Take the bus from Les Haudères to Villa (also spelt Villaz). Alternatively, you can start from and return to Evolène, which will add a further 1hr 15min to reach Villa.

From the bus stop walk back 20m to the yellow sign. Turn left and head up between buildings, then kink right and turn left past a water trough after 25m. Head up the paved road, which soon becomes a track. A track bears left but keep straight on, and straight on again where a path joins from the right after 10min.

Traverse left, in and out of trees, and then climb to cross the **Torrent des Maures**. Turn right at a sign and zigzag (a familiar theme on this walk) to arrive at

Flower-covered house in the hamlet of Villa

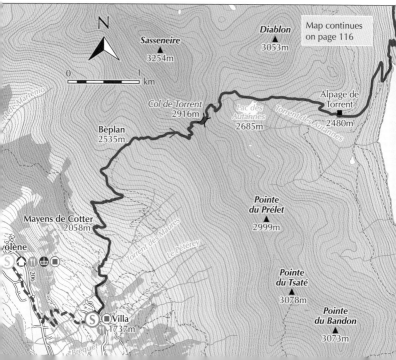

Map continues on page 116

N

0   1 km

Sasseneire
▲ 3254m

Diablon
▲ 3053m

Col de Torrent
2916m

Lac des
Autannes
2685m

Alpage de
Torrent
2480m

Torrent des Autannes

Bèplan
2535m

Pointe
du Prélet
▲ 2999m

Mayens de Cotter
2058m

Torrent des Maures

le Pèterey

Pointe
du Tsaté
▲ 3078m

ölène

206

S

Pointe
du Bandon
▲ 3073m

S ☐ Villa
1737m

Breguet

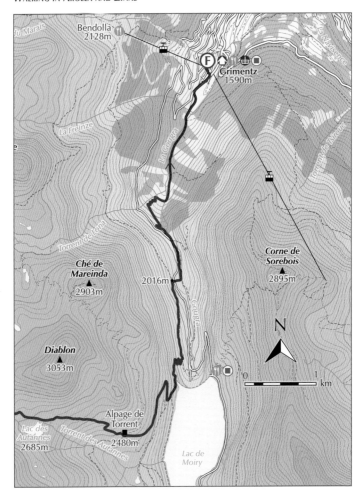

a track by a chalet. Go round the hairpin bend and continue across grassy meadows to arrive at the alp buildings at **Mayens de Cotter** (2058m, 50min).

After 40m on the track, head right and uphill, a large cross is directly above. The path begins an initial 400m climb in zigzags. Avoid a path headed left (our route is signed right) and get your head down for the climb, which is punctuated with windsocks, large rocks and another cross. Eventually, the route starts to climb a rib. Pass a couple of farm buildings at **Bèplan** on the left and come to a small lake (2535m, 2hr).

Continue up, the path now becoming a red-and-white route rather than a yellow route. It initially steepens before traversing under a peak and making the final ascent to the **Col de Torrent** (2916m, 3hr).

OPTIONS FROM THE COL DE TORRENT

North is the Sasseneire at 3254m, nearly 350m above, although it looks a lot less. It's definitely a Grade 4 route for experienced scramblers and mountaineers, initially over steep, outward sloping shale, then along the ridge. Allow 1hr up and 45min down.

South, at 2999m, is the Pointe du Prélèt. Again, one for mountaineers as it scrambles over the crest at nearly 3000m. The grade is beyond the walkers' scale in this book. Guides suggest 2hr 30min and similar in return.

Looking down from the Col de Torrent over the Lac des Autannes and the Lac de Moiry

Approaching the Moiry barrage on the descent from the Col de Torrent. The route up the Sorebois is across the Lac de Moiry

To continue to Moiry and Grimentz, descend the eastern slopes. Steep at first, the path is good and soon steadies, passing the large **Lac des Autannes** (2685m). Continue down, passing the **Alpage de Torrent** (2480m, 3hr 50min). Keep heading down on a grassy path to the left of the track and keep left at a junction in 5min with the contouring 2500m path (Walk 26). Continue down to the west end of the Moiry barrage. Refreshments and buses are available at the café across the barrage.

From the barrage continue down on the Grimentz path. After a few zigzags below the barrage, the path becomes rough for 1km as it descends steadily. Cross the road at **2016m** and continue for 50m to the stream (La Gougra) and turn left just before it. Continue steadily down, staying close under the road. Touch the road by a bus stop and keep right. A long zigzag descent takes wide loops before arriving at **Grimentz** by the cable-car station (1590m, 6hr 15min).

FROM EVOLÈNE

From the centre of the village, walk south and past the Co-op supermarket (8min). After a further 300m, turn left on Route 214, which climbs on a good path, its sunken lane showing how old the path is. Climb past the cliffs above Evolène and via ferrata signs. At L'Omâzo, take the path doubling back to the left and follow this as it becomes a road into Villa. Allow 1hr 15min for the ascent and 45min if used in descent.

WALK 20

La Sage to Cabane de Moiry via Col du Tsaté

Start	La Sage (1668m)
Finish	Cabane de Moiry (2826m)
Distance	11.5km
Total ascent	1700m
Total descent	550m
Grade	3
Time	6hr
Max altitude	2868m at the Col du Tsaté
Refreshments	Possible summer buvette near Lac de Châteaupré
Access	Bus from Les Haudères to La Sage or walk from Evolène; bus from Parking du Glacier at head of Lac de Moiry

Along with the other crossings – the Pas de Lona and the Col de Torrent – of the long ridge between the Val d'Hérens and Val de Moiry, this route adds to the special valley-to-valley character of walking in the area. The Col du Tsaté, the hardest if not the highest of the three, is steep on both sides, but there are no difficult passages. The climb to the Cabane de Moiry is interesting throughout, initially on a moraine before a steeper final climb with a couple of cabled sections. The route follows a stage of the Haute Route, so you are likely to have company. Moiry is a spectacular cabane looking out over the Moiry glacier and icefall. If you want to stay overnight, which is highly recommended, book in good time as it can get busy. Walk 27 continues to the Barrage de Moiry and buses, or over the Sorebois col to Zinal.

From the centre of La Sage, walk down the road and 50m after the Restaurant L'Ecureuil, bear left on a lane. Rise through woods and, after zigzags, keep left at a sharp hairpin. Climb to the alp buildings at **Mayens de Motau** (1925m, 40min). From here there are views of the Dent Blanche and the Ferpècle glacier, as well as the Veisivi peaks across the valley.

Climb above the hamlet and the track becomes a path. Keep uphill alongside a stream and shortly cross it and climb to more alp buildings at **Le Tsalè**

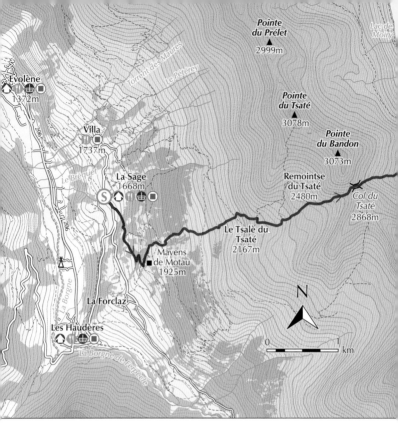

The small lake passed near the Remointse du Tsaté, with views to the
Aiguilles Rouges (right), Mont Blanc de Cheilon and the Pigne d'Arolla

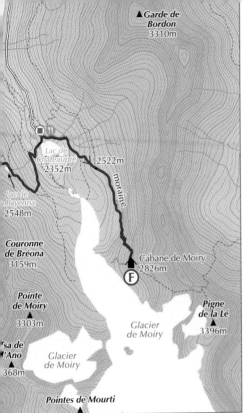

du Tsaté (2167m, 1hr 10min). Continue uphill on a steep path, crossing a farm track and reach the farm buildings of the dairy at **Remointse du Tsaté** (2480m, 2hr).

Turn right on a track, then veer left on a small path looking down on a small tarn in a bowl. Keep left and climb to a second bowl and then, after a crucifix, a third bowl with the Col du Tsaté above. Cross the stony bed of the valley and rise on the left-hand hillside on rockier ground to the **Col du Tsaté** (2868m, 3hr 30min). The best views – both up and down valley – start lower down.

The **Val de Moiry** runs from the glacier and icefall in the south to the Lac de Moiry, often a very bright blue, to the barrage, and then down to the village of Grimentz. With the Grand Cornier hidden away at the end, the views are very fine and the walking even more so.

The top of the descent is steep and crosses screes and shale before reaching grass. Views emerge of the Moiry icefall, with the cabane on top of rock slabs left of the icefall. Drop down to a tarn, the **Lac de la Bayenna** (2548m). Head right and after 500m swing left, avoiding paths that climb to the left bank of the Moiry glacier. Descend, initially on steep zigzags, to the roadhead (parking, bus, seasonal buvette) at the **Lac de Châteaupré** (2352m, 4hr 30min).

Pass the buvette on a track signed to the Cabane de Moiry, which becomes a footpath and rises onto the east side of a lateral moraine. At 1km from the buvette,

121

Looking towards the Moiry icefall from the Lac de Châteaupré, near the summer buvette

the path carrying the 2500m Tour du Lac de Moiry (see Walk 26) joins our ascent path. Around 40min after the buvette, slope down into a little ablation valley before climbing in zigzags, with two small sections of cables, up rocky slopes that lead directly to the **Cabane de Moiry** (2826m, 6hr).

The **cabane** looks out over the glacier and icefall, with full-length windows making the most of the views. Owned by the SAC, the hut was modernised and extended in 2010 and has beds for 96 people. Surrounded by peaks, it gives access to a range of climbing routes on the peaks and the glacier, as well as alpine walking routes to the Val d'Anniviers, which come out near the Cabane du Petit Mountet.

WALK 21

Evolène to Cabane des Becs de Bosson

Start	Evolène (1372m)
Finish	Cabane des Becs de Bosson (2982m)
Distance	11.5km
Total ascent	1710m
Total descent	100m
Grade	2–3
Time	5hr
Max altitude	2982m at the Cabane des Becs de Bosson
Refreshments	Buvette at L'A Vieille and the cabane at the finish

This walk, Stage 4 of the Tour du Val d'Hérens, starts in charming Evolène and climbs for most of a day to reach a high cabane with spectacular views, with an excellently sited buvette just over halfway. It's certainly a good test of uphill technique, but there is plenty of interest along the way to ease the undoubted rigours of the climb. And the views are truly worth the effort.

Unless you are continuing to Grimentz directly the same day (Walk 24 in reverse), you will likely overnight at the cabane so book ahead and take the necessary overnight gear.

From the centre of Evolène head north and after 3min turn right soon after the Hotel Hermitage. In a further 3min cross the main road that bypasses Evolène and head up a lane straight opposite. After 15min come to the Route de Volovron. Cross this and climb on the path, but soon join a track which climbs steadily. Paths make shortcuts so take them where marked. After 50min pass a cross and continue on the track to the hamlet of Le Berzo. From here continue ahead to the next hamlet, which is **Volovron** (1760m, 1hr 15min).

Turn right, signed to L'A Vieille, and head steeply uphill behind the buildings. Pass a chalet (Nid d'Aigle). After climbing 100m (15min) follow path signs left (1865m). Head into deep woods (the Ban de Volovron) on a path that is initially level but which soon alternates steepness with extreme steepness as it heads up. After 2hr 30min leave the forest to new views down valley to Sion and across to the Pointe de la Tsevalire. Contour the hillside and drop briefly to cross a stream.

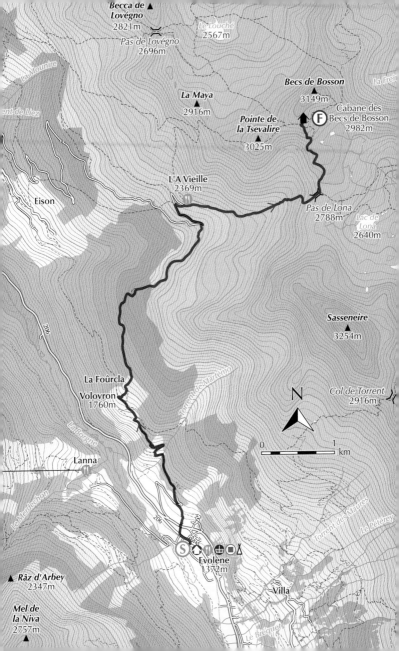

Becca de
Lovégno
2821m

Pas de Lovégno
2696m

Le Louché
2567m

La Maya
2916m

Becs de Bosson
3149m

Cabane des
Becs de Bosson
2982m

F

Pointe de
la Tsevalire
3025m

L'A Vieille
2369m

Pas de Lona
2788m

Lac de
Lona
2640m

Eison

Sasseneire
3254m

Col de Torrent
2916m

La Foûrcla
Volovron
1760m

La Borgne

N

0   1
|_____| km

Lanna

Râz d'Arbey
2347m

S

Evolène
1372m

Villa

Mel de
la Niva
2757m

Looking down to the Pas de Lona with the Mattertal peaks behind. The cabane has spectacular views

At a track, turn left. After 10min take a right-hand turn that climbs across pasture and comes to the farm and buvette of **L'A Vieille** (2369m, 3hr 10min).

After treating yourself – you might have been able to time your arrival for lunchtime – rejoin the path that climbs above the farm and passes under a small church. Initially fairly level, the path steadily steepens as it climbs above a bowl of pasture. It keeps steepening all the way to the **Pas de Lona** (2788m, 4hr 20min).

The col opens a spectacular vista, with the Weisshorn directly ahead and the Moiry valley below.

From the col turn left and climb eroded paths, dropping down 40m at one point and making the final steep climb, aided by a few lengths of chain, to reach the **Cabane des Becs de Bosson** (2982m, 5hr).

From the hut it's possible to explore further. Left is the 3025m **Pointe de la Tsevalire**, reached in about 20min without difficulty. From here there are stunning views into the Réchy valley, which Stage 5 of the TVH will explore, if you're making the full tour. To the right is the traverse to the **Col des Becs**

de Bosson. An alpine route up the pinnacles of the Becs de Bosson is possible from here.

THE CABANE DES BECS DE BOSSON

The cabane was originally built in 1997 and enlarged in 2012. It is owned by enthusiasts of the Société de la Cabane des Becs de Bosson, and it sleeps 62. Access from Grimentz, Moiry, Evolène and the Réchy valley ensures there are many trekking opportunities.

Water supply is limited (non-existent, really) so no showers or washing, and it is necessary to buy drinking water.

The views from the hut are spectacular, from the Weisshorn, the glaciers above Arolla and right round to the Dents du Midi in the west. It's a place for sunsets and dawns.

MULTI-DAY ROUTE
Tour du Val d'Hérens (TVH)

Start	Thyon (2096m)
Finish	Nax (1264m)
Distance	77.7km
Total ascent	4210m
Total descent	5050m
Time	27hr (5 days)

The Tour du Val d'Hérens (TVH) is a five-day route that makes a U-shaped tour of the Val des Dix and the main Val d'Hérens. The route covers 77km, climbs 4200m and drops 5000m. It combines remote walking, over the first two and last two days, with a gentler section between villages in the upper valley on Stage 3.

Thyon is a ski resort accessed by bus from Sion and Vex or gondola lift from Veysonnaz, but is, perhaps, best approached on the first morning bus for an early start. From Nax buses drop to Sion. Bus transport options are also available at the Dixence barrage, Arolla and throughout the Val d'Hérens.

Accommodation is mainly in small valley hotels, with a high hut at the end of Stage 4. Other hut and dorm possibilities are off-route, and there are several campsites along the route.

There are no resupply options except in the Val d'Hérens, between Arolla and Evolène.

The sections of the route are also described as day walks and the brief stage notes here should be read with those route descriptions in mind.

Stage	Start	Finish	Distance	Time	Ascent	Descent
1	Thyon	Grande Dixence barrage	17.5km	6hr	780m	740m
2	Grande Dixence barrage	Arolla	18.0km	6hr 30min	1170m	1300m
3	Arolla	Evolène	17.0km	5hr	450m	1090m
4	Evolène	Cabane des Becs de Bosson	11.5km	5hr	1710m	100m

Stage	Start	Finish	Distance	Time	Ascent	Descent
5	Cabane des Becs de Bosson	Nax	13.7km	4hr 30min	100m	1820m
			77.7km	27hr	4210m	5050m

STAGE 1

Thyon to Grande Dixence barrage

Start	Thyon (2096m)
Finish	Grande Dixence barrage (2138m)
Distance	17.5km
Total ascent	780m
Total descent	740m
Time	6hr
Description	See Walk 1

This stage forms a long traverse at around 2200m above the Val d'Hérémence, with views across to the peaks above Arolla and Pic d'Artsinol, which divides this valley from the main Val d'Hérens, and ahead to the Lac des Dix. The only refreshments are at the delightful Cabane d'Essertze after 2hr. After the initial walk out of the ski resort, there is a great feeling of space and remoteness on paths and

The superb balcony route heading south towards the huge Dixence barrage

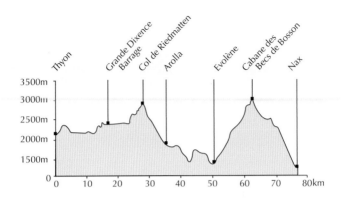

occasional short sections of track across open hillsides. The route crosses small, sporadic boulder fields but nothing difficult or exposed. As the route crosses the desolate Prafleuri Combe, there is a final climb to a high point before it drops to the base of the barrage.

Accommodation is in the Hotel du Barrage (The Ritz!), an unlikely-looking building originally built for workers on the vast dam, Europe's highest. But inside, beds and food await and both are good. Those with spare energy could continue up to the Prafleuri refuge, but book ahead as this is likely to be busy with Haute Route trekkers.

STAGE 2

Grande Dixence barrage to Arolla

Start	Grande Dixence barrage (2138m)
Finish	Arolla (2008m)
Distance	18km
Total ascent	1170m
Total descent	1300m
Time	6hr 30min
Description	See Walks 2 and 3

This stage passes through wild and remote country with no facilities on the route unless you divert to the Cabane des Dix, where it is possible to split the stage if desired. It's a fine day's walking with the vast lake, intricate terrain, moraines, high passes and a beautiful descent with the Dent Blanche ahead.

A climb to the dam is followed by a long, flat walk on the dam-side track then a climb above the lake into the upper Dix valley. Turn left for Arolla and cross to the next valley either by the awkward shale on the Col de Riedmatten or on the moraine and then ladders on the Pas de Chèvres before the steady descent to Arolla and welcome refreshments, resupply and transport if needed.

Accommodation could be at the Dix hut (so splitting the stage into two and adding a day to the TVH). In Arolla there is a range of mainly small hotels, some with dormitory accommodation, and a campsite nearby.

STAGE 3
Arolla to Evolène

Start	Arolla (2008m)
Finish	Evolène (1372m)
Distance	17km
Total ascent	450m
Total descent	1090m
Time	5hr
Description	See Walks 9, 10 and 14

The official route takes the gentlest route down valley to Les Haudères and then digresses to a series of attractive high villages above (the rock villages – La Forclaz, La Sage and Villa) before dropping to Evolène, the largest village in the valley and one of Switzerland's most unspoilt and pretty villages. Accommodation can be found in all of the villages except Villa, so many different plans are possible, but bear in mind that Stage 4 is a 5hr/1700m climb. Evolène has a range of hotels and a campsite.

There are also a number of possible diversions from the route after Arolla, some of which may be seen as improvements. A direct, high-level route (see Walk 10) stays high above the valley on the Arolla side and eventually drops directly into Evolène, following Swiss Route 6 all the way. It is also possible to follow this route to the beautiful Lac Bleu and descend to join the main route at La Gouille (see Walk 9) and then follow the valley route to Les Haudères and from where there are numerous possible routes between Les Haudères and Evolène.

STAGE 4
Evolène to Cabane des Becs de Bosson

Start	Evolène (1372m)
Finish	Cabane des Becs de Bosson (2982m)
Distance	11.5km
Total ascent	1710m
Total descent	100m
Time	5hr
Description	See Walk 21

This Stage of the TVH starts in charming Evolène and climbs for most of a day to reach a high cabane with spectacular views, with an excellently sited buvette just over halfway. It's certainly a good test of uphill technique but there is plenty of interest and reasons to stop along the way. And the views are truly worth the effort.

An attractive alpage and buvette at L'A Vieille after 3hr 15min seems preordained as a lunch stop before the final climb to the wide Pas de Lona and final steep pull to the remote cabane; other than this there are no facilities on the route.

The cabane is in a wonderful location, with views south to most of the main peaks of the Valais – Weisshorn, Zinalrothorn, Ober Gabelhorn, Dent Blanche and Pigne d'Arolla, but not the Matterhorn. If you arrive in good time, the walk up the Tsevalire peak takes 45min up and down, while the scramble up the alpine route to the Becs de Bosson summit would need 2–3hr.

STAGE 5
The Cabane des Becs de Bosson to Nax

Start	Cabane des Becs de Bosson (2982m)
Finish	Nax (1264m)
Distance	13.7km
Total ascent	100m
Total descent	1820m
Time	4hr 30min
Description	See Walk 22

This final stage of the Tour du Val Hérens explores part of the protected and undeveloped Val de Réchy before crossing an easy col and making a long (1250m) descent, mostly in beautiful woods, into the spread-out village of Nax, which has spectacular views over Sion and the Rhone valley as well as mountains to the north and south.

The upper section of the route is wild and remote, with the beautiful Le Louché lake as a centrepiece. Small-scale skiing on Mont Noble doesn't detract from the stage, but the descent into Nax is long, over 1500m of downhill, and a bit of care is needed to keep to the marked trail in the forest into Nax.

There are no facilities on the route until Nax, where there is a café and bus transport to Sion and from there back into the main valleys if desired.

VAL D'ANNIVIERS AND VAL DE MOIRY

The Weisshorn towers above the Arpitettaz valley seen from the route to the Cabane du Petit Mountet on Walk 28

Crossing a stable section of boulders and scree, with spectacular views of the 4000m peaks at the head of the valley (Walk 33)

Running south from the small town of Sierre (Siders in German), the Navisence river carves a deep gorge, rising quickly to nearly 1000m at Vissoie, a strategic village where all public transport to the other villages in the Val d'Anniviers coordinates in a hub. Perched on sunny terraces above Vissoie are the resorts of St Luc and, higher and further north, Chandolin. The main Val d'Anniviers continues to rise beyond Vissoie, passing through the hamlets of Mission and Ayer to reach the resort of Zinal surrounded by mountains, including four 4000m peaks – the Dent Blanche (4357m) (shared with the Val d'Hérens), the Ober Gabelhorn (4063m), the Zinalrothorn (4221m) and the Weisshorn (4505m) (shared with the Mattertal and Zermatt).

The western Val de Moiry branch is guarded by the resort of Grimentz where the Gougra river valley to the south leads up to reach the Moiry barrage and its encircling mountains. From the Grand Cornier (3961m), two ridges run northwards, cradling the Moiry valley, each with a succession of peaks and high passes providing the walker and trekker with routes west to the Val d'Hérens. A series of high huts around the valley provide climbers with access to the peaks but also destinations for walkers, whether day trips or overnight stays. A well-known tour of the high cabanes visits the Moiry valley and three high huts in the upper valley south of Zinal, and can be completed within a week.

RÉCHY VALLEY

WALK 22

Cabane des Becs de Bosson to Nax

Start	Cabane des Becs de Bosson (2982m)
Finish	Nax (1264m)
Distance	13.7km
Total ascent	100m
Total descent	1820m
Grade	2–3
Time	4hr 30min
Max altitude	2982m at the Cabane des Becs de Bosson
Refreshments	None on the route
Access	Take Walk 21 to the Cabane des Becs de Bosson. From Nax take buses to Sion and to valley destinations

This final stage of the TVH explores part of the protected and undeveloped Val de Réchy before crossing an easy col and making a long (1250m) descent, mostly in beautiful woods, into the village of Nax, which has spectacular views over Sion and the Rhône valley as well as mountains to the north and south.

From the cabane head slightly down to the **Col de la Tsevalire** (5min), passing cairns and statues of the virgin. The col has good views ahead into the Val de Réchy, and its geological melange is clear to see with sinkholes and outcrops of chalky rock. From the col take the clear path through the rocks. The first 200m are steep before the path levels somewhat and then drops again to the path junction at **Le Louché lake** (2567m, 50min).

Continue down from the lake, and after 5min keep left where the Route 217 Val de Réchy path divides. Follow this over hummocky ground until you approach a small lake (the **Gouille de la Grand-Rionde**, 2468m), but before this take a path left above the lake, signed to the Col de Cou. The path traverses the hillside before

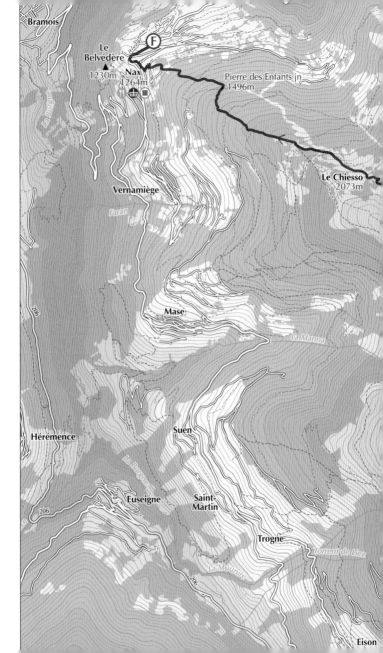

Bramois

Le
Belvédère
▲
1230m

Ⓕ

Nax
1264m

Pierre des Enfants jn
1496m

Le Chiesso
2073m

Vernamiège

Faran

Mase

La Manna

Suen

Hérémence

La Borgne

Euseigne

Saint-
Martin

Trogne

Torrent de Liez

La Moumie

Eison

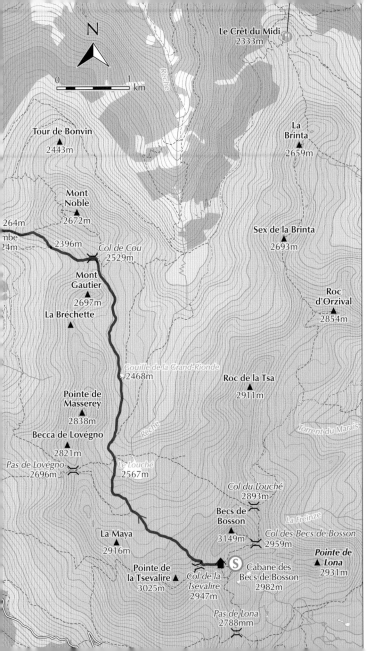

Le Crêt du Midi
2333m

N

0   1
km

Tour de Bonvin
2443m

La Brinta
2659m

Mont Noble
2672m

264m
nbe
24m

2396m

Col de Cou
2529m

Sex de la Brinta
2693m

Mont Gautier
2697m

La Bréchette

Roc d'Orzival
2854m

Gouille de la Grand-Rionde
2468m

Roc de la Tsa
2911m

Pointe de Masserey
2838m

Becca de Lovégno
2821m

Reche

Torrent du Marais

Pas de Lovégno
2696m

Le Louché
2567m

Col du Louché
2893m

La Freinze

Becs de Bosson
3149m

Col des Becs de Bosson
2959m

La Maya
2916m

Pointe de Lona
2931m

S   Cabane des Becs de Bosson
2982m

Pointe de la Tsevalire
3025m

Col de la Tsevalire
2947m

Pas de Lona
2788mm

rising gradually to the **Col de Cou** (2529m, 1hr 50min). It is possible to make an ascent of Mont Noble from here. Nax is signed as 2hr 30min from here for the 1250m descent.

Descend from the col on a path initially disturbed by grazing cows and goats. Keep left at a 2396m junction and pass under the Mont Noble ski lift and close by a farm building to reach a junction at **La Combe** (2324m, 2hr 15min).

Continue ahead for Nax. Cross an area that can only be described as a heather moorland before dropping into the top of the forest. There are few turns but Nax is straight ahead. Cross four tracks at roughly 1930m, 1790m, 1710m and 1600m before coming to the **Pierre des Enfants** junction at 1496m and merging with Swiss Route 58, the Chemin des Bisses.

> **Bisses** are an ingenius irrigation system used in the Valais and throughout the Alps. Water is moved along channels, often many centuries old, alongside the path, to where it is needed.
>
> The Chemin des Bisses runs from the Col des Planches near Martigny to Grimentz in the Val d'Anniviers in a trail of over 100km. There is no evidence of a bisse on this short section into Nax, although water pipes lie beneath.

Follow this down. It becomes a road, then after a bend the route heads down on a track named the Route de Leigier, which drops down to another road. The centre of Nax is laid out below, so follow the waymarks to reach the bus stop, with a restaurant close by, in **Nax Centre** (1264m, 4hr 30min).

If using public transport, you will need to take the bus, almost certainly via Sion, to return to the main centres in the Val d'Hérens.

Coming into the village of Nax, high above Sion

WALK 23
Réchy valley

Start/finish	Le Crêt du Midi (2333m)
Distance	15km
Total ascent	650m
Total descent	650m
Grade	2
Time	5hr
Max altitude	2567m by Le Louché lake
Refreshments	Le Crêt du Midi and buvette at Tsartsey; the Cabane des Becs de Bosson is 1hr 10min off-route
Access	Bus to Vercorin from Sierre, then gondola from Vercorin to Le Crêt du Midi. The route (with extra time, ascent and distance) could be done from the Cabane des Becs de Bosson

The Réchy valley is well protected, tucked between the Val d'Hérens and the Val d'Anniviers and facing north to the river Rhône. It is one of Switzerland's few remaining blanket peat bogs, 90 per cent of which have been lost over the last 150 years. The valley is awkward to access from anywhere except Vercorin and the Crêt du Midi lift, so it takes a special trip, which will be well rewarded with almost complete wildness, a range of birds and animals, flowers and the results of what appears to have been a geological mixing machine, ranged across a series of four hanging valleys.

From Vercorin, take the gondola lift to **Le Crêt du Midi**, a small ski area with a sizeable café. From the exit, head south, downhill, for 2min before climbing for another 3min. Keep right at a path junction. Continue through trees and across rocky slopes to a junction with a track at **2177m** (35min).

Turn left on the track. This passes above the forests of the lower slopes of the Réchy valley. Pass under the **Buvette de Tsartsey** (or stop a while, as you wish). Pass an entrance barrier into the protected area and after a few more metres come to a path junction at **2204m** (1hr).

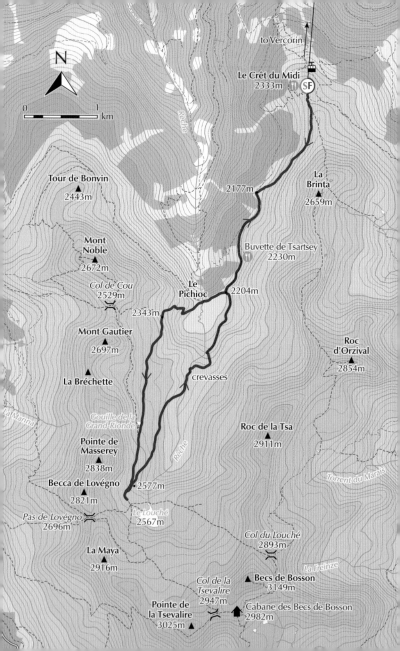

to Vercorin

Le Crêt du Midi
2333m SF

La Brinta
2659m

Tour de Bonvin
2443m

2177m

Mont Noble
2672m

Buvette de Tsartsey
2230m

Col de Cou
2529m

Le Pichioc

2204m

2343m

Mont Gautier
2697m

Roc d'Orzival
2854m

La Bréchette

crevasses

Gouille de la Grand-Rionde

Roc de la Tsa
2911m

Pointe de Masserey
2838m

Becca de Lovégno
2821m

2577m

Torrent du Marais

Pas de Lovégno
2696m

Le Louché
2567m

Col du Louché
2893m

La Maya
2916m

La Freinze

Col de la Tsevalire
2947m

Becs de Bosson
3149m

Pointe de la Tsevalire
3025m

Cabane des Becs de Bosson
2982m

Peaks surrounding Le Louché lake

Here is a **moment of choice**: which way to do the loop. Each way has its advantages: to the left the route climbs quickly to the most beautiful part of the valley, so if you think you might need to curtail the walk, this is the way to go. But heading right gets the climbing out of the way sooner, and is the way described.

Turn right and in 10min come to **Le Pichioc** (2183m), a fine viewpoint from were paths head down valley. To the south, a large expanse of marshland is the first evidence of the protected blanket bog. But keep left and climb, passing a turn to the Col de Cou at **2343m** after 1hr 30min. Keep left again and traverse and climb steadily. This part of the route has the feel of a Scottish moor, or that of a peatland, save the fact that it is 2000m higher with rocky pinnacles above.

Pass a small lake with a big name (the **Gouille de la Grand-Rionde**, 2468m) and continue to work your way gradually up. Join up with the descent path, and 5min later arrive at the beautiful **Le Louché lake** tucked in a mountain bowl (2567m, 2hr 40min).

If you have time and energy, or are planning an overnight at the **Cabane des Becs de Bosson**, there are two options to reach it from this point. A route left heads over grass then scree to the Col du Louché, and then contours behind the Becs de Bosson summit to reach the cabane in 1hr 45min and 450m of ascent; this is a Grade 3 route. A quicker route goes straight ahead to the Col

de la Tsevalire, also climbing steep scree but on an easier path, reaching the Cabane des Becs de Bosson at 2982m in 1hr 10min from Le Louché lake.

To head down valley, retrace your steps from the lake to the path junction 5min downhill. Keep right on a descending path that looks out over the Réchy stream. After passing above some boggy ground, come to a beautiful area of small trees, humps of rocky moraine and numerous picnic spots. Signs warn of '**crevasses**' – in this case, small holes in the ground. Cross the river which veers into a deep gorge – the gap is all of 10cm, but don't fall in. Continue downhill to arrive at a track and small water-management building. Continue on the track, past the gates and **buvette**. At 2177m turn right and follow the path back to **Le Crêt du Midi** (2333m, 5hr).

MOIRY VALLEY

WALK 24
Grimentz to Cabane des Becs de Bosson

Start	Grimentz cable-car station (1590m)
Finish	The Cabane des Becs de Bosson (2982m)
Distance	9km
Total ascent	1430m
Total descent	40m
Grade	2
Time	4hr 30min
Max altitude	2982m at the cabane
Refreshments	Bendolla station then none until the cabane
Access	Bus to Grimentz

The Cabane des Becs de Bosson stands at nearly 3000m, between Grimentz and Evolène. It is the first hut in the TCVA but also a good objective for a day walk from Grimentz or the Bendolla gondola station above the village.

The hut is well sited and has comfortable facilities, but as with many high huts it lacks a reliable water supply – no showers or even running water here. But standing well back from the peaks, it has some of the finest views of the range, including all the main Zinal peaks and most of those above Evolène and Arolla too. An overnight stay for the sunset and sunrise is recommended.

The ascent is a walk of three parts. The lower half is on pleasant grassy hillsides, while the upper section crosses an area turned over to ski-industry needs. The last half hour follows mountain paths below the imposing Becs de Bosson.

From Grimentz, take the signed path by the Bendolla gondola station. The path grinds uphill beneath the happy tourists in the ascending gondolas above. Pass a beautiful chapel and continue the climb, now off to the north of the lift, arriving

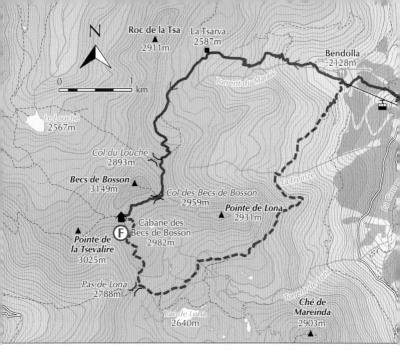

at the **Bendolla station** (2128m, 1hr 30min). If time is short, or pride and common sense allow, take the gondola and rise effortlessly up the 540m ascent in under 10min.

The initial climb above Bendolla is on grassy slopes

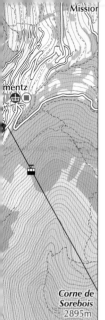

From the gondola station, with its restaurant, play area and ski training areas marked off, head right and after 20m find the signed path to the left. It crosses a flat area before heading uphill. Soon you pass the last of the ski facilities and the route becomes a pleasant climb on a well-made path up the grassy hillside. Arrive at **La Tsarva ski lift** (2587m) with Bob's restaurant (not open in the summer) in 1hr 20min from Bendolla.

Turn left, now on a track servicing the higher ski facilities. After 20min find a signed path to the right and take this as it contours round the disturbed mountainside. Meet the track again and head away after 100m, then climb to the junction with a path leading to the **Col du Louché** (2893m), an entry into the protected Réchy valley. Turn left, now on a narrow path that climbs through rubble from the ragged Becs de Bosson peak above (reached by an alpine trail for those looking for more ascent). The strange pipe you see coming out of the mountain is a pressure-driven avalanche-management system. Cross the **Col des Becs de Bosson** (2959m) and continue for 15–20min to reach the **Cabane des Becs de Bosson** (2982m, 4hr 30min from Grimentz, 3hr from Bendolla).

As well as spectacular views, there are **two easy peaks** close by: the Pointe de la Tsevalire is an easy walk, but the Becs de Bosson requires some mountaineering skills. It's a fine place and well worth the walk.

Direct descent to Grimentz

The quickest return route is to retrace your steps to Grimentz, taking about 2hr to Bendolla and 3hr to Grimentz.

Descent by the Pas de Lona

This more interesting route back to Bendolla takes only 15–30min longer than the direct return. From the cabane descend steep ground to the **Pas de Lona** (2788m, 30min). There are a couple of chain sections immediately below the hut, and a small kick-up in the middle of the descent. The ground by the wide pass is cut up, showing its underlying sandstone hereabouts. Turn left at the Pas de Lona, left again at a junction after 10min, passing above the Lac de Lona, and bear left again at a third junction 20min later. The route skirts below the summit rocks of the **Pointe de Lona**, turns over a ridge and drops more gently to **Bendolla**. From the Pas de Lona, the return route to Bendolla follows Route 6.

WALK 25

Cabane des Becs de Bosson to Cabane de Moiry

Start	Cabane des Becs de Bosson (2982m)
Finish	Cabane de Moiry (2826m)
Distance	16.7km
Total ascent	850m
Total descent	1000m
Grade	3
Time	5hr 30min
Max altitude	2982m at the start
Refreshments	Possible summer refreshments at the Lac de Châteaupré
Access	Routes to the Cabane des Becs de Bosson from Evolène (Walk 21) or from Grimentz (Walk 24)

Taking in the second stage of the TCVA, this varied walk heads towards the glaciers around Moiry, which are in view for most of the walk. With the turquoise Lac de Moiry below and the tumbling icefalls above, it is an arresting scene, a trekker's wonderland.

There are no real difficulties on the route, which could be split by using transport at either end of the Lac de Moiry. There is a choice of routes: the official TCVA, which heads along the shoreline of the Lac de Moiry, or an option along the 2500m contour round the lake, which takes a little longer but is more interesting walking with better views.

From the Cabane des Becs de Bosson, drop down to the **Pas de Lona** (2788m, 30min). The sandy terrain has been much eroded while the vast piles of rubble and rock on the flanks of the Sasseneire, directly ahead, hint at its glaciated past. Turn left and keep right at another junction in 5min, where Route 6 heads away towards the Pointe de Lona and Bendolla gondola station for Grimentz. Continue down past the Lac de Lona, at the end of which turn right at a junction at **2641m** (50min).

From here the route is a good track, little used by vehicles but possibly by cyclists. Climb to the pass at the **Basset de Lona** (2791m, 1hr 30min). From here it's a 30–40min round trip to climb the nearby Ché (or Sex) de Mareinda (2903m), which gives fine views over the entire Moiry valley.

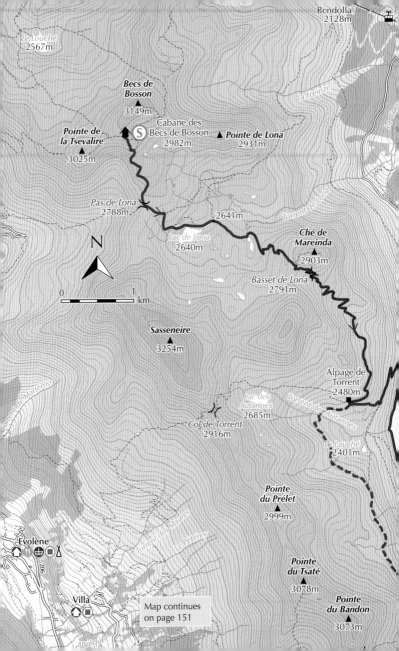

Le Louche
2567m

Bendolla
2128m

La Freinze

Becs de
Bosson
3149m

Cabane des
Becs de Bosson
2982m

Pointe de
la Tsevalire
3025m

Pointe de Lona
2931m

Torrent de Lona

Pas de Lona
2788m

2641m

Ché de
Mareinda
2903m

N

Lac de Lona
2640m

Basset de Lona
2791m

0   1 km

Sasseneire
3254m

Alpage de
Torrent
2480m

Lac des
Autannes
2685m

Torrent des Autannes

Col de Torrent
2916m

Le Lauché
2401m

Torrent de Marênno

Pointe
du Prélet
2999m

Évolène

Le Peterey

Torrent des Maures

Pointe
du Tsaté
3078m

Villa

Map continues
on page 151

Pointe
du Bandon
3073m

Le Brequet

The Lac de Lona – the past course of the glacier is clear to see

Continue down the track which twists and turns, although there are plenty of shortcuts. After 30min pass a high farm building. Throughout the descent the views to the icefall and the culminating Dent Blanche become bigger and better. Come to the farm at **Alpage de Torrent** (2480m, 2hr 30min). Continue below the alp on a grassy path to reach a junction in 5min.

Here there is a choice:

- Either keep descending on Route 6 towards the barrage. After reaching a track, continue down to the lake and after a few metres, turn right to continue along the lakeshore, and then onwards to the parking at the head of the valley and **Lac de Châteaupré** (2352m, 4hr).
- Or, recommended in good weather, turn right on the path that contours around the Lac de Moiry at 2500m. This meets the route descending from the Col du Tsaté before looping down to reach the parking and lake. This takes about 30min longer but has the better views and walking (see Walk 26).

From the parking, pass a small summer buvette and start the climb to the Cabane de Moiry. Climb along a narrow moraine, sometimes in the ablation valley alongside. Keep right at a junction at **2522m**, shortly dropping into the ablation valley, then climb in zigzags and through a couple of short sections with cables for protection to reach the **Cabane de Moiry** (2826m, 5hr 30min).

A modern extension has been grafted onto the traditional **cabane**, largely subsuming it, but the new building is among the most stunning cabanes in the Alps, with great facilities and a vast picture-window view over the Moiry icefall. The cabane is on the Chamonix–Zermatt Haute Route, so if you're planning to stay overnight, it's best to book ahead.

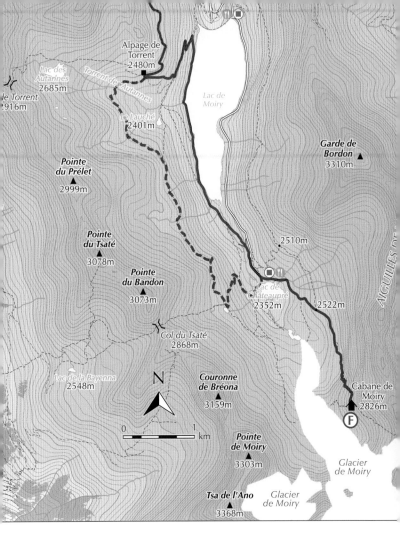

To return from the Cabane de Moiry, either follow Walk 27 to Zinal or return to the parking by the lake, where buses run to Grimentz.

WALK 26
Lac Moiry circuit 2500m

Start/finish	Moiry Barrage (2250m)
Distance	14.2km
Total ascent	630m
Total descent	630m
Grade	2
Time	5hr
Max altitude	2590m
Refreshments	Moiry barrage; seasonal buvette at Lac de Châteaupré
Access	Postbus from Zinal and Grimentz; car parking

This is a great walk full of interest and dramatic scenery throughout. Lying between the Val d'Hérens and Val d'Anniviers, the head of the Moiry valley leads south towards the Moiry glacier with its dramatic icefall, overlooked by the Cabane de Moiry, a favoured overnight stop for trekkers on the Chamonix–Zermatt route.

The path above the eastern shore undulates for much of the time at around 2500m. The views of the Moiry glacier and the peaks beyond come late – but are worth the wait! The western path has more open views towards the Moiry icefall, and apart from one short, exposed section, there is little to choose between in terms of the direction for this walk. If time is pressing, there is an option to walk just half and return by bus.

From the car park and bus stop at the barrage, take the path, signed to Sorebois and Zinal, rising away from the barrage to join a track and continue uphill through seven hairpin bends. At the eighth hairpin continue ahead on the rising track, heading south. The track soon becomes a path, continuing to rise across the grassy hillside, crossing several gullies, to reach a rise at (2540m, 1hr). The path continues at around this height, then crosses a much deeper gully to come to the eastern shore high point of **2555m** (1hr 30min).

The path continues to undulate gently at around the 2500m height until finally, after 2hr, a magnificent view opens up: the Moiry glacier and icefall set in a bowl surrounded by snow-capped peaks. Continue for a further 10–15min,

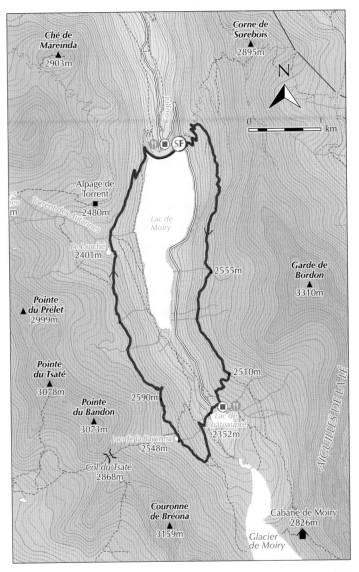

Ché de
Mareinda
▲2903m

Corne de
Sorebois
▲2895m

N

0 ——————— 1
km

Gougra

🍴 🅿 SF

Alpage de
Torrent
■2480m

Torrent des Autannes

Lac de
Moiry

Le Lauché
2401m

2555m

Garde de
Bordon
▲3310m

Pointe
▲du Prélet
2999m

Pointe
du Tsaté
3078m

Pointe
du Bandon
▲3073m

2590m

2510m

🅿 🍴
Lac de
Châteaupré
2352m

Lac de la Bayenna
2548m

Col du Tsaté
2868m

Couronne
de Bréona
▲3159m

Cabane de Moiry
■2826m

Glacier
de Moiry

AIGUILLES DE LA LÉ

153

Walkers get their first good views of the Moiry glacier and icefall

then turn right at a path junction at **2510m** and head down to **Lac de Châteaupré** (2352m, 2hr 30min). Paths to the left here head to the Cabane de Moiry (see Walk 25).

Cross the bridge over the outflow of the lake. The route leads directly ahead through two hairpin bends now on a track, then reverting to a path to climb onto the lateral moraine, still heading south. The way then turns right off the moraine, crossing a small stream and then continuing steeply up the hillside to join a path now heading north. Climb steadily to come to **Lac de la Bayenna** (2hr 20min) – a beautiful tranquil spot at the foot of the path from the Col du Tsaté.

From the lake, climb to a rocky high point with a large cairn at **2590m** (3hr 30min). Take care negotiating the steep path as it descends then climbs over the rocky rib. A short section of chain is reassuring at one point. The way quickly becomes easier, undulating across pastures at around the 2500m height. Begin descending to reach a small lake at **Le Lauché (2401m)**, then just after, join a track which rises slightly then descends through two hairpins. (The descending path from the Col de Torrent joins here.) Fork right on a signed path for the final descent to cross the dam, noting information boards related to the hydro scheme and the surrounding mountains and glaciers. Return to the bus and car park area, with a restaurant just above.

WALK 27
Cabane de Moiry to Zinal

Start	Cabane de Moiry (2826m)
Finish	Zinal (1674m)
Alternative finish	Sorebois (2437m)
Distance	16km
Total ascent	720m
Total descent	1870m
Grade	2–3
Time	6hr 30min (4hr 30min to Sorebois)
Max altitude	2840m at the Corne de Sorebois
Refreshments	Restaurant by the barrage; various Sorebois cable-car stations; café at the main 2437m station above Zinal
Access	One of several routes from (or to) the Cabane de Moiry

This walk from the Cabane de Moiry to Zinal follows the Chamonix–Zermatt Walker's Haute Route and the third stage of the TCVA. It assumes an overnight stay in the Cabane de Moiry.

The descent from Moiry is steep but without problems. The traverse above the Lac de Moiry undulates among rocky outcrops and may feel quite long, while the climb to the Corne de Sorebois follows a good path. From this high point it's about 1200m down to Zinal, but this can be avoided, if desired, by taking a gondola from the higher Espace Weisshorn/Vouarda station or the Sorebois station. Descent to Grimentz is also possible from the Espace Weisshorn station.

Descend from the cabane, reversing the previous day's climb. After 40min, at a junction at **2522m**, keep right on a contouring path and keep right again at another junction at **2510m** after 1hr.

From here the route traverses high above the Lac de Moiry, the path weaving and undulating over the rocky terrain of the steep mountainside to find the best route. It may feel longer than expected, but any tiredness will be quickly offset by looking back at the valley behind, while a range of interesting peaks ahead around the Becs de Bosson (see Walks 21–25) invite interest, if you haven't

Corne de Sorebois
2895m ▲

La Vouarda/Espace
Weisshorn station

2837m

Sorebois
2437m

2374m

Zinal
1674m

Garde de
Bordon
▲
3310m

N

0 _____ 1
km

2510m

Lac de
Châteaupré

2522m

moraine

Cabane du Petit Mountet
▲
2140m

Cabane de Moiry
2826m

S

Glacier
de Moiry

uronne
Bréona
3159m

Pointe
de Moiry
▲
3303m

Pigne de la Lé
▲
3396m

Glacier
de Moiry

Tsa de
l'Ano
Glacier
de Moiry
3368m

Looking ahead to the Moiry icefall from the end of the Lac de Moiry

explored there yet. The path starts to descend and eventually meets the path rising from the Barrage de Moiry at **2374m** (2hr 20min).

Turn right and climb the steep but reasonably graded path to the slight dip in the ridge by the **Corne de Sorebois** (2837m, 3hr 40min). This divides the Moiry spur from the main Val d'Anniviers, and the new views of the Weisshorn and Zinalrothorn will accompany your descent to Zinal.

You have been on Route 6 since meeting the path above the barrage. Continue on this, dropping past the higher **Espace Weisshorn** station (refreshments). Unless you are lured by the attractions of the gondolas, continue down to the **Sorebois station**, with more refreshments and more gondolas (2437m, 4hr 30min).

To reach Zinal, head 5min past the Sorebois restaurant and find a small path to the left. Initially a little unclear, this is the main path to Zinal and has been much improved in recent years. (An alternative descent would be to take the continuing track, reaching Zinal in a similar time.) Pass under the gondola, sparing a moment to pity or envy those in the swinging cars. The descent is on Route 6, so continue down, keeping right at path junctions. As it enters woods, the path is an amazing construction of innumerable tight zigzags. Compared with the vertical plunge of the old path, this is close to heaven.

Join with a path that has risen from Mottec and keep right under the gondola lines. Zinal is visible just below. Pass a picnic area, come to a bridge and make the short climb into **Zinal** (1674m, 6hr 30min).

ZINAL

WALK 28
Zinal to Cabane du Petit Mountet

Start/finish	Zinal (1674m)
Distance	13km
Total ascent	620m
Total descent	620m
Grade	1–2
Time	4hr 30min
Max altitude	2247m at Plan de Lée
Refreshments	Cabane du Petit Mountet (2140m); La Tsoucdanna, at the end of the Zinal road
Access	Bus to Zinal

This is a fine introductory walk or familiarisation trip for those planning routes to the higher huts in the upper Val d'Anniviers. There are three paths to the cabane and this walk uses two of them in ascent and descent, although the nearby track is also a good walk too. From the hut and trails there are fine views of the Weisshorn, the Zinalrothorn, the Pointe de Zinal at the head of the Glacier de Zinal, which the cabane overlooks, and the Grand Cornier at 3961m.

From the centre of Zinal, take the old 'Vieux Zinal' road rather than the newer main road and continue past old chalets before passing two gites and then descend a little to join the road at the parking and last bus stop (20min).

Cross the **bridge** and turn left. Signs explain the importance of the Lée pastures here and higher above. Cross the flat pasture and come to another bridge in 45min. Keep right and climb on a good track. Pass signs to the **disused copper mine** (a 30min digression but only visitable with a guide – enquire at the tourist office). Five minutes after this, and 20min from the start of the climb, take a right turn shortly before the **Vichiesso** buildings that show the life of the pastoralists, including cheese-making.

Climb on grass and after 5min take a second turn right (the onward path will be our descent route). This path climbs steeply at first through woods and eventually onto open hillside. As you climb, the Arpitetta cirque comes into view and soon after the Weisshorn, the highest peak around the valley at 4505m.

At 2145m pass a small path left signed to the cabane but don't take this turn. Continue to the junction with the Sorebois path at **2247m** after 2hr.

The path contours and descends gradually before dropping more steeply to the **Cabane du Petit Mountet** (2140m, 2hr 30min).

The original **family-owned hut**, built in 1899, burned down and has since been rebuilt several times. At 2–2hr 30min from Zinal it makes a perfect first-hut experience. Sleeping 40 in small dorms, it has great views from its position high on the moraine.

The fine views across and up the valley continue, with a peep at the Glacier de Zinal and a hint of the rigours of the path to the higher Cabane du Grand Mountet on the slopes of Besso, across the glacier (see Walk 29).

From the cabane, descend steeply and at the first path junction, keep straight ahead unless you want to descend by the track. Continue on steadily rockier ground and through an ablation valley before coming into woods. The path stays steep and stony, and at 1910m comes to a brief cabled section. Merge with the ascent path and in a few minutes come to the descending track near **Le Vichiesso** (3hr 25min).

Continue down, pass the bridge and then cross pasture and the second bridge before keeping right above the new road and taking the old way straight back into **Zinal** (4hr 30min).

After the flat walk up the valley, the route starts to climb near some large boulders. The peak is Besso

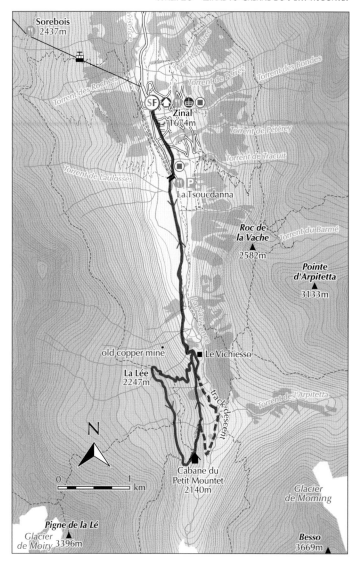

Sorebois
2437m

Torrent des Roch...

Torrent de Perré

Torrent des Bondes

SF

Zinal
1674m

Torrent de Pétérey

Torrent de Tracuit

Torrent de Laulosses

La Tsoucdanna

Roc de
la Vache
2582m

Torrent du Barmé

Pointe
d'Arpitetta
3133m

La Navisence

old copper mine

Le Vichiesso

La Lée
2247m

track descent

Torrent de l'Arpitetta

N

0   1
⊢――――――――――⊣ km

Cabane du
Petit Mountet
2140m

Glacier
de Moming

Pigne de la Lé
Glacier
de Moiry 3396m

Besso
3669m

WALK 29

Zinal to Cabane du Grand Mountet

Start	Zinal (1674m)
Finish	Cabane du Grand Mountet (2886m)
Distance	11km (22km round trip)
Total ascent	1290m (1370m round trip)
Total descent	80m (1370m round trip)
Grade	3–4
Time	5hr (9–10hr round trip)
Max altitude	2886m at the cabane
Refreshments	Cabane du Petit Mountet, 30min off-route
Access	Bus to Zinal

This is a great walk, probably the sternest in this guide. The scenery is dramatic, the path is excellent and the going hard. After a gentle walk up the valley, the route crosses a bridge and begins a steep climb on the flank of Besso, looking down over the Glacier de Zinal and the Cabane du Petit Mountet. The long route along the flank of Besso is followed by a section of chains before a slow stretch across scree and boulders to reach the hut.

The scenery is dramatic. The Dent Blanche stands supreme behind the Grand Cornier followed by the shapely Pointe de Zinal. The Ober Gabelhorn hides until near the hut approach. After the hut a 5min extension gives even closer views of the glaciers and the Zinalrothorn, and paths from the viewpoint can take the walker even closer to the glaciers and climbing routes.

Unless you are a very strong walker, it's not recommended you tackle this in one day. It's only slightly quicker to descend than climb, so the round trip would likely be 9–10hr. This gives you a great opportunity to overnight in a high mountain hut alongside climbers preparing for their routes the next day.

Leave Zinal on the old road. At the **car park** after 15min cross the Navisence river and take the well-worn track across the pastures of Lé. It seems to be flat but by the end, after 30min, you will have ascended the first 70m.

Sorebois
2437m

Les Diablons
3609m

Diablon des Dames
3538m

Torrent des Bondes

Torrent de Peroc

Torrent des Rocheres

Zinal
1674m

Torrent de Peterey

Torrent de Tracuit

La Tsoucdanna

Torrent de Barmé

Roc de la Vache
2582m

Torrent de Lauflosses

Pointe d'Arpitetta
3133m

Le Vichiesso

Cabane Arpitettaz
2786m

Navisence bridge
1900m

Torrent de l'Arpitetta

Cabane du Petit Mountet
2140m

† 2582m

Pigne de la Lé
3396m

Besso
3669m

Glacier de Moming

cier
oiry

Blanc de Moming
3661m

N

0   1
km

Map continues on page 164

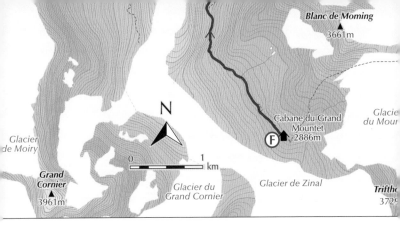

By the boulders keep right on the track and climb past the buildings and water supply at **Le Vichiesso**. Continue along the track and come to a **two-humped bridge** over the Navisence river. Take this and turn right. The walk along the river is a gentle introduction to what is to come.

After 5min the path begins to climb. Soon it joins a moraine with views down to the remains of the glacier and across to the Petit Mountet cabane. After 25min the path turns left and climbs very steeply under a rocky buttress. Although it leaves the buttress, it continues with roughly the same abrupt gradient as it climbs onto the open mountainside of Besso. The route levels out and turns definitively up valley, with a couple of short sections with rope guidance, and comes out by a **cross** after 2hr 35min.

Looking ahead on the trail with the Dent Blanche (behind) and the Grand Cornier across the Glacier de Zinal

Spectacular even if diminished, the glaciers and peaks at Grand Mountet, with the Dent Blanche right and Pointe de Zinal in the centre

From here on, the already rugged route becomes more so. Traversing at 2500m, cross a couple of streams and soon come to a **Himalayan-style bridge** that crosses a chasm. After another traversing section, the route starts to climb on a good path cut through rocks and well protected by chains. Climb up a further 200m before the path levels out with a view of the Ober Gabelhorn.

From here on, there is limited climbing but almost the entire route is on a boulder field. Take care to stay on the waymarked trail, which is as good as possible in this terrain, but progress is inevitably slow. Eventually the **Cabane du Grand Mountet** comes into view, a short distance ahead.

Situated in the heart of a mountain cirque, the location of the **cabane** is riveting, fully justifying the effort of the climb. It's a large hut, taking 90 in dortoirs (dormitories), but it's busy with climbers and walkers so if you want to stay overnight, book in good time. The secretive Ober Gabelhorn directly faces the hut, its north face a Grade D (difficult) climb. To the left, the rocky 'other side' of the Zinalrothorn takes pride of place, while to the right the Pointe de Zinal and Dent Blanche dominate. All around the glaciers, much reduced but still dramatic, flow from the peaks.

To return to the valley means reversing the route. Familiar from the ascent, the route will still take some time. Allow 3hr to reach the Navisence bridge, although signs and maps suggest quicker times. Familiarity may make the route seem easier, but ensure you stay on route through the boulder fields; if you stray even 5m off-route it's possible to lose all signs of the marked path. The chained section likewise may feel easier.

From the Navisence bridge, reached in about 3hr, cross and continue right past **Le Vichiesso**. Continue to the valley floor and on to **Zinal** in a further 1hr 15min.

WALK 30
Roc de la Vache from Zinal

Start/finish	Zinal (1674m)
Distance	15km
Total ascent	940m
Total descent	940m
Grade	2
Time	5hr 30min
Max altitude	2582m on the Roc de la Vache
Refreshments	None on the route until 1km from the end, at La Tsoucdanna
Access	Bus to Zinal

This walk was author Kev Reynolds' favourite in the entire Valais region and it's easy to understand why. It climbs on good paths high above Zinal, a route shared with Walk 31 to the Cabane de Tracuit. From the Roc de la Vache the views of the Glacier de Zinal, Grand Cornier and Dent Blanche are sublime. And as you descend the narrow path from the Roc, the Moming Glacier, Zinalrothorn and, later in the descent, the Weisshorn come into view. The route takes a similar time and has a comparable level of challenge from the Arpitetta side, which has the advantage of returning you directly to Zinal, but the way described here gives better views as you descend.

From the centre of Zinal, by the 'Centre Ville' bus stop, take the old road past chalets. Pass the Hotel Les Bouquetins and turn left on Tracuit into the **Reka holiday village**. Immediately take a narrow track on the left which climbs above the village. If you miss this, pass in front of the buildings and rejoin at the second hairpin. Climb on the road and take the path signed to the right at the third hairpin.

An alternative start is from the Plan de la Lée parking area. Take a poorly signed path at the north end of the parking and follow it into woods, past a small chalet and up. Circuit around a drainage control area for the Tracuit stream before joining the main route at the hairpin turn off.

Climb a little and merge with a track. Keep an eye open for the path making a left turn after 10min. The path and the track interweave as they climb the hillside,

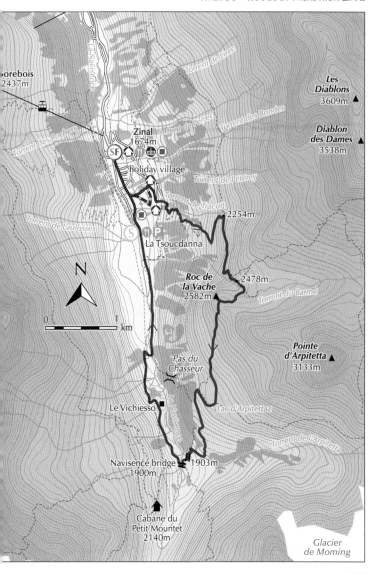

both heading to the 2254m path junction. Initially, the path climbs above the ravine gouged by the Torrent de Tracuit, then continues steadily through woods before emerging onto open hillside at 2050m and a group of farm buildings. Continue climbing on the path, which is occasionally steep but well made. Come to a path junction at **2254m**, where a traversing path from the north joins. (This path, which comes from the Hotel Weisshorn, may be closed as it is exposed to stonefall.)

Turn right. The path is mainly level until it climbs again through a rocky section on a well-made trail. In places there are options. The main path is signed but the paths all rejoin. The path levels out and comes to a junction at **2478m**. The path to the left continues to the Cabane de Tracuit (see Walk 32), nearly 800m above at 3259m.

Descend a little to cross the Torrent du Barmé on a good bridge. Climb steadily to reach a shoulder. The **Roc de la Vache (2582m)** (2hr 45min) is 50m to the right. Views from the Roc include the entire valley: across the Rhone to the Wildstrubel range, the Grand Cornier and the Dent Blanche.

The descent route passes the Lac d'Arpitetta, under the Weisshorn and Zinalrothorn

Climb over a metal stile, perhaps the hardest obstacle on the route. The path initially keeps left near rocks but gradually emerges onto open hillside, passing the disused Tsijère de la Vatse building and then continuing onwards, but less steeply, to the delightful **Lac d'Arpitettaz (2229m)** (3hr 25min). Views up the Arpitetta valley to the Weisshorn are spectacular.

Turn right here and soon descend an attractive moraine. The path heads south again and passes a turn to the alpine-graded Pas du Chasseur, which shaves 20min from the descent time. Continue down and come out first at the bridge over the **Torrent de l'Arpitetta** and then a bridge over La Navisence stream.

Turn immediately right, signed to Zinal. After 15min pass the **Vichiesso** exhibit on pastoral life in the valley and the higher pastures. Continue down and then on either side of the river (left across wide pastures, right over the bridge on a good track). Pass the parking at the end of the valley and continue, turning right onto the outward road and then past old chalets into the centre of **Zinal** (5hr 30min).

WALK 31

Cabane Arpitettaz from Zinal

Start	Zinal (1674m)
Finish	Cabane Arpitettaz (2786m)
Distance	11km (22km round trip)
Total ascent	1155m (1200m round trip)
Total descent	45m (1200m round trip)
Grade	3
Time	4hr 30min, 3hr 30min return, about 8hr round trip
Max altitude	2786m at the cabane
Refreshments	Cabane du Petit Mountet, 20min off-route
Access	Bus to Zinal

The Cabane Arpitettaz is a small refuge nestled below the rocks and glaciers of the Weisshorn and Zinalrothorn, affording an up-close view of these famous peaks. At 8hr walking, the round trip makes a long day but can readily be split over two days with an overnight stay in the welcoming cabane.

The route presents few issues under good conditions, but it is quite long for a single day unless you are acclimatised at over 2000m. If overnighting, consider an approach over the Roc de la Vache (see Walk 30), adding 1hr to the ascent. If comfortable with alpine-grade trails, a return over the Col de Milon adds a further 1–1hr 30min to the descent and could also take in the Cabane de Tracuit (see Walk 32).

From the centre of Zinal take the Vieux Zinal route, passing the houses and barns, reaching the **parking** area in 15min. Cross the Navisence river and walk along the flat pastures of the Lé to reach the end of the valley. (It's quite possible but less attractive to stay on the track on the right bank of the river, crossing at the point where the path starts to climb. The track side is shaded in the mornings and may be cooler in hot weather.) Those with alpine skills might try the Pas du Chasseur, a blue route that climbs steeply and directly to just below the Lac d'Arpitettaz, saving 30min overall.

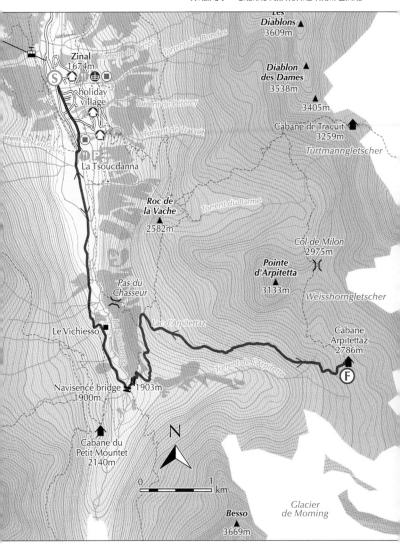

Les
Diablons
3609m

Diablon
des Dames
3538m

3405m

Cabane de Tracuit
3259m

Turtmanngletscher

Zinal
1674m

S

holiday
village

P

La Tsoucdanna

Torrent de Petérey

Torrent de Tracuit

Torrent des Bondes

Roc de
la Vache
2582m

Torrent du Barmé

Col de Milon
2975m

Pointe
d'Arpitetta
3133m

Weisshorngletscher

Pas du
Chasseur

Lac d'Arpitettaz

Cabane
Arpitettaz
2786m

F

Le Vichiesso

Torrent de l'Arpitetta

Navisence bridge
1900m

1903m

N

Cabane du
Petit Mountet
2140m

0   1
└──────┴──────┘ km

Besso
3669m

Glacier
de Moming

Passing a number of large boulders, start the climb on the good track. Pass the buildings at **Le Vichiesso** after climbing for 20min, and after a further 20min reach the two-humped **Navisence bridge** (1900m, 1hr 10min).

Cross the bridge and keep left, rising and dropping again to cross the Torrent d'Arpitetta close to a gushing waterfall. Climb the sloping path for 15min before emerging onto pastures. You may find flocks of sheep guarded by patou dogs in this area, so go around the flocks if possible. If approached by the dogs, stay calm while they confirm you are not a threat.

Keep climbing, with the Pas du Chasseur route joining from the left. The path curves right and continues along a narrow moraine to come to the **Lac d'Arpitettaz** (2229m, 2hr 20min).

The **tiny tarn** is a much-visited spot on a sunny day and a delightful place to stop before the rest of the climb. Views along the Glacier de Zinal and the peaks above, and up the Arpitetta valley fully justify its popularity.

Above the lake the path is joined by the route descending from the **Roc de la Vache** and continues gradually uphill for 1km. Thereafter, it climbs slightly cut-up ground with various path options before levelling out at 2500–2600m. Cross a bridge over a stream and climb the final 200m to the **Cabane Arpitettaz** (2786m, 4hr 30min).

Almost surrounded by the peaks, the **cabane** is in an enviable location. With only 24 beds, it's important to reserve a spot if you wish to stay overnight.

Descent is by the same route, taking 3hr 30min unless you opt to tackle the Col de Milon or return over the Roc de la Vache to **Zinal**.

The small Cabane Arpitettaz is a welcoming hut in a spectacular location

WALK 32

Cabane de Tracuit from Zinal

Start	Zinal (1674m)
Finish	Cabane de Tracuit (3259m)
Distance	9km (18km round trip)
Total ascent	1600m (1620m round trip)
Total descent	20m (1620m round trip)
Grade	3
Time	4hr 45min ascent; 3hr 15min descent; total about 8hr
Max altitude	3259m at the cabane
Refreshments	None on the route
Access	Bus to Zinal

The Cabane de Tracuit is the highest in the valley at over 3250m and the round trip can be done in one long day or split with an overnight at the cabane. The climb is long and without problems, although a short, chained section on rocks to reach the hut will challenge some, but this is easier than it first appears.

The hut is in a spectacular position, right on the col with dramatic mountain views. It's a main start point for climbing the Weisshorn so will be busy with climbers who will make an early start. As well as its location, the modern hut is superbly equipped and has a magnificent viewing window as well as a range of small dorms.

Leave Zinal on the Vieux Zinal route, past old houses. At the **parking** turn left on a poorly signed path. This climbs between trees and then crosses a fence before climbing above water-management constructions. At one point the path meets a road and turns away immediately. Climb the narrow and zigzagging path, taking care to avoid the track climbing alongside, where warning signs indicate you should avoid it. Pass a cross and come to the small group of farm buildings of Le Chiesso (2065m, 1hr 30min). (Alternative starts are possible through the Reka holiday village. Either keep left at the entrance on a gravel track and join the path later or pass in front of the buildings to meet it sooner.)

The Col de Milon, with the Zinalrothorn and Dent Blanche on the horizon

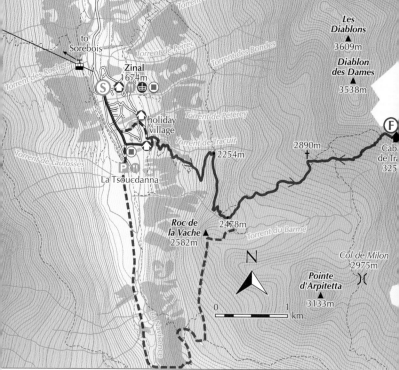

Climb on the good path with broadening views of the Glacier de Zinal and the peaks above. At **2254m** come to a path junction and turn right. This traverses south for about 1km before climbing through cliffs on a good path to come to a junction at **2478m** (2hr 30min). (The route so far is the same as Walk 30 to the Roc de la Vache, for which turn right.) From here on, the cabane can be seen high on the ridge ahead; some will find this inspiring, others less so!

For the cabane keep left. It's over 2hr to the hut from here and virtually every step is up. After 15min pass a small summer farm building and continue up. The route makes a series of steps before levelling off and climbing again.

At 2950m pass a turn signed to the Col de Milon. This is an alpine route between Tracuit and the Cabane Arpitettaz – the shaley col can be seen. But keep heading up. The path steepens in small zigzags before coming to a final rocky step with good footholds and well protected by a cable. On the narrow col, turn right for 100m to reach the **Cabane de Tracuit** (3259m, 4hr 45min).

The **views** are stunning. Ahead is the Weisshorn (4505m), with the Tête de Milon ahead and then glaciers heading towards the Bishorn (4151m). The jagged ridge of the Weisshorn leads past the awkward-looking Grand Gendarme (4097m) standing high above the ridge. Left and down is the Turtmanntal, a quiet valley with a couple of huts and the hamlet of Gruben, well known to Haute Route trekkers. To the right the peaks fight for attention, the Zinalrothorn and Dent Blanche the most prominent. From here, unusually, it's possible to spot the secretive Ober Gabelhorn and, lurking behind the Pointe de Zinal, the summit of the shy Dent d'Hérens. Mount Blanc can even be seen further west.

The **cabane** is stunning too, a recent construction with fabulous window views and small comfy dorms. An overnight is recommended, although the route can be done in a long (about 8hr) walk, plus breaks. An early start would be needed.

To return to the valley it's a question of retracing your steps, with a full 1600m of downhill. Take care over the rocky section and head steadily down on the remarkably good path, doubtless passing others heading upwards. Allow about 2hr to the 2478m junction and 1hr 15min from there to **Zinal**.

Alternative finish
If you overnighted at the cabane, a return over the Roc de la Vache is suggested, one of the finest viewpoints in the region. Either descend to the 2478m junction and turn left and climb back or find a shortcut about 30m above this turn. Climb for 30min to the Roc. And having absorbed the closer views of the peaks

The glacial approach to the Weisshorn at the Cabane de Tracuit

surrounding the Glacier de Zinal, head down, reach the delightful small tarn of the Lac d'Arpitettaz. From here drop down to the bridge, turn right, passing Le Vichiesso after 15min and continuing to **Zinal** (3hr from the 2478m turn).

The cabane is as modern inside as it is from the outside

HOTEL WEISSHORN AND CHANDOLIN

WALK 33

Chandolin, Planets Trail, Hotel Weisshorn to Zinal

Start	Chandolin (1979m)
Alternative start	Tignousa (2184m)
Finish	Zinal (1674m)
Distance	20km (16km from Tignousa)
Total ascent	650m
Total descent	950m
Grade	2
Time	6hr 15min (5hr 15min from Tignousa)
Max altitude	2424m
Refreshments	Tignousa; Hotel Weisshorn
Access	Bus to Chandolin, or funicular from St Luc to Tignousa

This route combines the opportunity to visit the legendary Hotel Weisshorn with a fantastic balcony route from the hotel all the way to Zinal. The entire route is waymarked with yellow 'Z' markings for a runners' challenge route from Sierre to Zinal, so there is little difficulty route finding. You will probably encounter runners training on various sections of the route.

This is a long walk, and you may prefer to start at Tignousa to save 4km. There is little difficulty, although the descent into Zinal is steep and hard on the legs at the end of a long day.

Beginning in Chandolin, take the path to the right of the tourist office, named the Chemin du Vieux Mélèze. Climb initially, then cross pastures under the Tsapé chairlift. Fork right, then briefly follow a rushing stream and branch left to climb through woods. The path undulates then crosses an open pasture before arriving at **Tignousa** (2184m, 1hr, refreshments).

Follow the signed track, passing below the observatory, and continue on an almost level track lined with information points related to the planets and solar

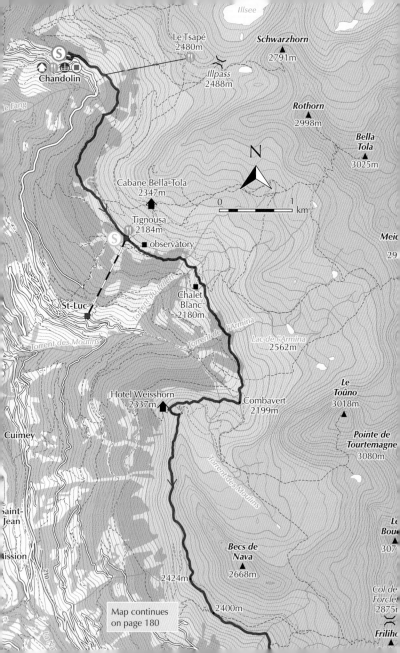

Chandolin

Le Tsapé
2480m

Schwarzhorn
2791m

Illpass
2488m

Rothorn
2998m

Bella
Tola
3025m

N

0   1
km

Cabane Bella-Tola
2347m

Meid

29

Tignousa
2184m

observatory

Torrent de Tsilette

Chalet
Blanc
2180m

Torrent de l'Armina

Lac de l'Armina
2562m

St-Luc

Le Fang

Torrent des Moulins

Cuimey

Hotel Weisshorn
2337m

Combavert
2199m

Le Toûno
3018m

Pointe de
Tourtemagne
3080m

Torrent des Moulins

Saint-
Jean

lission

Becs de
Nava
2668m

Le
Bou

307

2424m

2400m

Col de
Forcle
2875r

Map continues
on page 180

Map continues
on page 180

Frilih

Looking north across the hillside towards Chandolin, the Rhône valley far below

system. Arriving at **Chalet Blanc** (2180m), go up and take the path behind the farm buildings, which contours around the hillside, eventually joining the track that has followed a similar course below. Note that you should follow the track if you intend to stop at all the planet information stations. The track leads all the way around the hillside to another building and a junction of tracks at **Combavert** (2199m, 2hr).

FRANÇOIS-XAVIER BAGNOUD OBSERVATORY

Founded in 1995, this facility occupies an exceptional location, benefiting from both dark skies and generally good weather conditions. Its aims are to promote an understanding of astronomy to the wider public, and to provide facilities for amateur astronomers and researchers to conduct experiments and measurements. There are regular public sessions for astronomy and sun observations throughout the year, published on the website www.ofxb.ch.

The Planets Trail stretches from just below the observatory to Hotel Weisshorn. Various installations, including a giant sundial, and visual and audio features for each planet, are located at their relative locations on a scale of 1:1,000,000,000.

Take the first (lower) track, which soon passes 'Uranus', becoming a rising path, and cross the **Torrent des Moulins**, over a wooden bridge. The path to Hotel Weisshorn steepens and there are incredible views north to St Luc far below. Steadily climb to arrive at **Hotel Weisshorn** (2337m, 2hr 45min).

Hotel Weisshorn sits on a promontory above the Val d'Anniviers, with superb views mainly down towards Sierre in the Rhône valley below. Built by

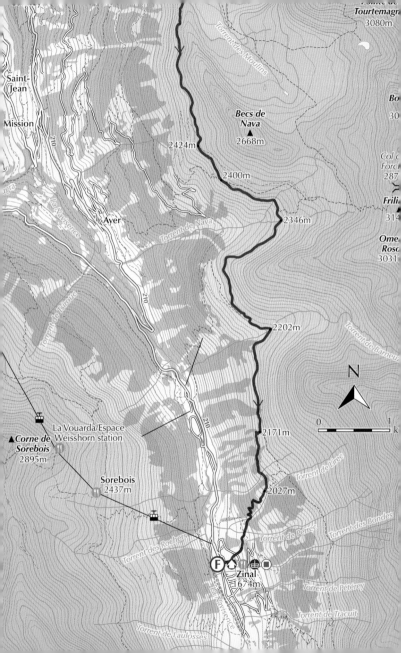

Saint-
Jean

Mission

210

La Navisence

Ayer

210

Torrent de Nava

Torrent des Moulins

Becs de Nava
▲
2668m

2424m

2400m

2346m

2202m

Torrent de Barneux

N

0   1
                    k

2171m

La Vouarda/Espace
Weisshorn station

210

▲*Corne de Sorebois*
2895m

Sorebois
2437m

2027m

Torrent de Lirec

Torrent des Rochers

Torrent de Peroog

Torrent des Bondes

F

Zinal
1674m

La Navisence

Torrent de Peterey

Torrent de Tracuit

Torrent de Laulosses

Pointe de
Tourtemagr
3080m

Bo
30

Col d
Forc
287

Frili
314

Ome
Rosc
3031

A superb balcony route heading south, with the Dent Blanche crowning the view

Francesco and Pierre Mosoni, the original hotel opened in around 1883 but was destroyed by fire. The current building was then constructed in 1891. It retains its vintage charms, but at a high price!

From the hotel take the track curving slightly uphill, then at a minor col (with 'Neptune' and 'Halley's Comet' on the top of the hill, now to the left) turn right onto a good path which rises towards an apparent high point. There is a bench here where you can enjoy the view back to the hotel. (The lower path directly from the hotel is less well maintained.) Continue along this wonderful balcony route, undulating and gradually gaining height. Pass the 'Pluto' sculpture, then cross above a small ablation valley with the remnants of a lake and continue to eventually join a track. To the right is a picnic area and a Swiss flag marking the highest point at **2424m** (3hr 45min).

Immediately fork right onto a path signed to Zinal. At the next path junction fork right again, now working your way around an enormous bowl in the hillside, descending very gradually all the while. Pass a signed path on the left directing walkers to the Col de Forcletta – one of the main passes used by trekkers walking from Chamonix to Zermatt on their way to Gruben. The views across to Grimentz and the Becs de Bosson above are spectacular, as are the views south to the head of the valley.

The path occasionally crosses scree and boulders, all very stable. Pass through a ranch-style entrance gate and keep behind the isolated alp building, continuing steadily down into a gully with a lively stream crashing down, only to be swallowed into a water system. Cross one larger scree and boulderfield. The path seems to cling to the hillside, reluctant to leave the fine views, but then at **2171m** (5hr 30min) branch right. The descent is steep all the way. First through pine woods, the path levels occasionally, with glimpses down to Zinal far below. Eventually come to a clearing by a chalet (water) and head right across pasture then into woods again. Pass through a tunnel under a rock to make the final descent into **Zinal**.

WALK 34
Bella Tola from Tignousa

Start/finish	Tignousa (2184m)
Distance	11.5km
Total ascent	880m
Total descent	880m
Grade	3
Time	4hr 30min
Max altitude	3025m on the summit of Bella Tola
Refreshments	Cabane Bella-Tola (2347m), 30min above Tignousa
Access	Bus to St Luc and funicular to Tignousa

This walk takes in one of the region's great viewpoints, the 3000m mountain of Bella Tola. Some distance from the main peaks, the summit of Bella Tola provides splendid views of the Weisshorn and many other peaks, as well as across the Rhône valley and west to the Grand Combin and Mont Blanc.

The walk starts from the top of the Tignousa funicular, which runs from 08:00, or it can be combined with an overnight either before or after the ascent at the Cabane Bella-Tola. Sunrise from the summit is said to be an experience not to miss. This route can be combined with a trip to the observatory and the Planets Trail, between the Tignousa station and Hotel Weisshorn (see Walk 33).

The walk includes a small but steep variant extension to give a different descent, which is recommended unless you have an aversion to steep scree.

From the exit of the funicular station, turn left and take the uphill path signed to Bella Tola and the cabane. Climb the zigzags to the **Cabane Bella-Tola** (2347m, 30min).

The **hut** was completely renovated in 2021 and has a large sunny terrace with all-encompassing views to the Weisshorn, Ober Gabelhorn, Matterhorn and Dent Blanche. It's a stunning spot for sunset and sunrise photos, as well as refreshments on the descent.

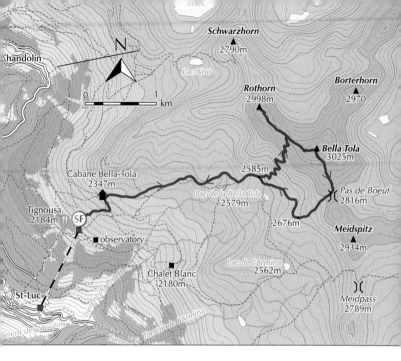

Climb directly above the hut on a good path. Join a track after 10min and turn left from it in 20min. The path climbs above the track and soon veers away, crossing streams before meeting the track again. Turn left uphill and come to a yellow sign at a junction at **2585m**, which marks the beginning of the steep ascent (1hr 20min). The zigzag path is directly ahead on the looming mountainside.

Climb the steep path that snakes up the hillside. There are many options, but the best path is usually clear and the least steep option. Just before you reach the ridge, pass a small hut which contains an 'Exposition Sierre–Zinal' honouring the famous mountain marathon. Climb above this, reaching a sign on the ridge (2928m, 2hr 15min).

For the **Rothorn** summit, turn left on the eroded path along the top of the fairly narrow ridge. To reach the viewpoint to the north allow 20min each way for the ridge climb to 2998m.

For Bella Tola turn right, initially along narrow paths with formidable views down the hillside just climbed and steep drops on your left. Various routes head to the summit of **Bella Tola** (3025m, 2hr 35min). There are 360-degree views, but

Rocky pinnacles on the Bella Tola ridge

it's the view south that dominates. To the west the peaks above Arolla, the Grand Combin and Mont Blanc range are clearly seen.

To descend there are two options:

- Return the way you came, back to the ridge junction and then the slopes so recently climbed, reaching the 2585m junction in around 45min, or
- descend the steep path directly ahead to reach the Pas de Boeuf, taking 30–40min.

Pas de Boeuf route

Drop off the alarmingly steep top. Soon find a rope indicating the descent, but better still, find the reasonable zigzags down the hillside. After 10min the scree descent bottoms out and the modest path crosses wild terrain, descending gradually to reach the **Pas du Boeuf** (2816m, 3hr).

Turn right and follow the track, which in places turns into a path. Bear right by some piste signs, and then right again on a track passing above the Lac de la Bella Tola, and another track that leads to it. After a further 3min come to the junction at **2585m**, where the steep ascent to the top began and where walkers taking the direct descent join (3hr 30min).

From here, continue down the track, turning right after a steep section and traversing the high pastures, crossing two streams and following the route to **Cabane Bella-Tola** (2347m, 4hr 25min). Continue down past the Cabane to the **Tignousa funicular station** (2184m, 4hr 45min).

WALK 35

Illhorn, Illsee, Lac Noir and Cabane Bella-Tola

Start	Le Tsapé (2480m)
Finish	Tignousa (2184m)
Alternative finish	Le Tsapé
Distance	10km
Total ascent	520m
Total descent	820m
Grade	2
Time	4hr
Max altitude	Illhorn (2717m)
Refreshments	Le Tsapé, Bella Tola, Tignousa
Access	Bus to Chandolin and from St Luc; Tsapé chairlift from Chandolin; funicular from Tignousa to St Luc

The ascent of the Illhorn is an opportunity to enjoy far-reaching panoramic views from Mont Blanc, across the Rhône valley, to the Bernese Oberland. It's an easy climb from the Pas de l'Illsee, the steady slope contrasting with the precipice on the northern side. Steep, stony paths lead to the Illsee, with an indistinct path crossing above the lake then up to Lac Noir.

Using the chairlift from Chandolin to Le Tsapé provides you with plenty of time (and energy!) to climb the Illhorn, and by combining it with using the funicular from Tignousa, there is ample time to explore the hillsides below the Rothorn and Bella Tola.

From the Tsapé chairlift, take the path behind the building at the back of the lift and climb easily, heading north. The path traverses the hillside then drops to reach the broad **Pas de l'Illsee** (2545m, 20min). Take the path directly ahead, which climbs at a steady gradient in a series of broad zigzags, and after a further 30min reach the summit of the **Illhorn** (2717m, 50min).

Views from this accessible peak are exceptional – to the west Mont Blanc is clearly visible, while to the south the view is dominated by the shapely Dent Blanche. Following further round are the Point de Zinal, Ober Gabelhorn,

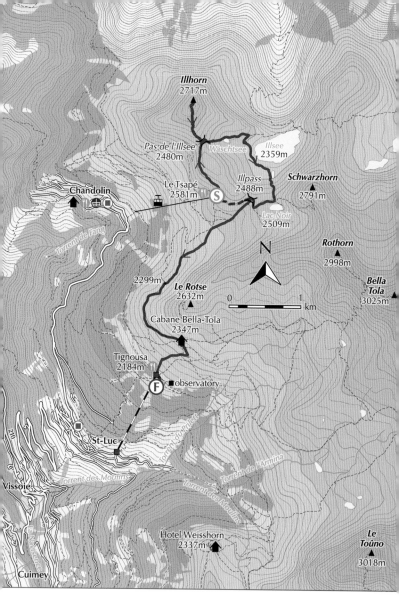

Illhorn
2717m

Pas de l'Illsee
2480m

Wäschtsee

Illsee
2359m

Le Tsapé
2581m

Chandolin

Illpass
2488m

Schwarzhorn
2791m

(S)

Lac Noir
2509m

Rothorn
2998m

N

Torrent de Fang

2299m

Le Rotse
2632m

Bella
Tola
3025m

0   1
km

Cabane Bella-Tola
2347m

Tignousa
2184m

(F) ▪ observatory

St-Luc

Torrent des Moulins

Torrent des Moulins

Torrent de l'Arnina

Vissoie

Hotel Weisshorn
2337m

Le
Toûno
3018m

Cuimey

The Illsee and the natural Wäschtsee, with the conical Schwarzhorn behind

Zinalrothorn, Weisshorn and Bishorn, all except the Point de Zinal being over 4000m.

Descend the way you came up, then at the Pas de l'Illsee turn left and descend steeply towards the lake below. The gradient eases as the route passes the natural **Wäschtsee** tarn. Cross a broad pasture to reach a path junction next to a building (2410m, 2hr). The route now follows the Sentier de la Chénégouga (chéné meaning oak). Initially crossing a pasture towards a broken-down wall, the path is indistinct but signed occasionally with red-and-white paint splashes and arrows. The path heads across the grassy hillside towards the prominent, conical Schwarzhorn. At a small lake below a scree slope the path becomes clearer, swinging right to climb steeply to **Lac Noir** (2509m, 2hr 20min).

Lac Noir is a popular spot for anglers and walkers alike, being easily accessible from Le Tsapé. The Schwarzhorn rises directly above, and an Alpine trail (blue waymarks) rises first to the south then directly north to the summit.

From Lac Noir follow the rising path directly to the Illpass and join a track. The **Illpass** is on a bend in the track. Take the small path down to the left, across a pasture, to meet a descending track from Le Tsapé at a hairpin bend. Continue down the track, then 10min from the Illpass take the less distinct track to the left, which quickly becomes a path to the left of a ski piste, with good views across to Chandolin and Sierre far below. Pass under a chairlift and enjoy the path as it now makes its way through boulders and a profusion of flowers, juniper and dwarf pines, descending to another track at **2299m** (3hr 40min).

Turn left. The track initially rises, then descends, gently heading south, with superb views up the Val d'Anniviers and across to Grimentz. Pass under a chairlift, then just before another chairlift, note the rising track at 2284m. To go directly to Tignousa simply continue on the descending track.

Although not signed, the rising track to the left leads directly in 10min to **Cabane Bella-Tola** (refreshments). This is a worthwhile detour at the end of the day, with fine views east to the peak Bella Tola (3025m) and the surrounding mountains.

To reach the Funicular at **Tignousa** from Cabane Bella-Tola, take the descending path below the refuge across pastures to reach the funicular in 20–25min.

From the bottom of the funicular at St Luc, turn right and walk down into the village. Bus stops are located on the main road just beyond the main square.

St Luc is less developed than Chandolin as a resort, and many older houses still cling to the hillside. The François-Xavier Observatory is located at Tignousa.

Alternative route
To return to Le Tsapé from the Illpass, keep on the track which descends gently to arrive 5min later. This makes a shorter walk of 6km and under 3hr.

Heading towards Tignousa on the track below Cabane Bella-Tola

MULTI-DAY ROUTE

Tour des Cabanes du Val d'Anniviers (TCVA)

This week-long tour takes in all the main high huts in the Val de Moiry and the Val d'Anniviers. The official route staging suggests seven days, although it should be achievable in six, but at the expense of missing a night in the Cabane de Tracuit.

The staging presented in official write-ups and followed here is designed as a trek staying overnight in the various cabanes, although this does lead to some slightly unbalanced stages. It would be possible to stay in Zinal, but this would miss out on the Cabane du Petit Mountet.

Most of the route is covered in the day walks, and these are referred to in the outline of the route. Note that other tours of the cabanes are written up elsewhere, but this follows the locally signed and published routing.

Stage	Start	Finish	Distance	Time	Ascent	Descent
1	Grimentz	Cabane des Becs de Bosson	9.0km	4hr 30min	1430m	40m
2	Cabane des Becs de Bosson	Cabane de Moiry	16.7km	5hr 30min	850m	1000m
3	Cabane de Moiry	Cabane du Petit Mountet	21.3km	7hr 30min	1170m	1860m
4	Cabane du Petit Mountet	Cabane du Grand Mountet	8.0km	4hr 15min	1100m	350m
5	Cabane du Grand Mountet	Cabane Arpitettaz	13.0km	6hr	990m	1090m
6	Cabane Arpitettaz	Cabane de Tracuit	10.0km	5hr	1170m	700m
7	Cabane de Tracuit	Zinal	9.0km	3hr 15min	20m	1610m
			87km	**36hr**	**6730m**	**6650m**

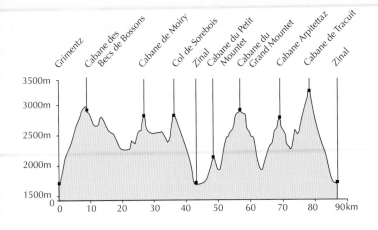

STAGE 1

Grimentz to Cabane des Becs de Bosson

Start	Grimentz cable-car station (1590m)
Finish	Cabane des Becs de Bosson (2982m)
Distance	9km
Total ascent	1430m
Total descent	40m
Time	4hr 30min
Description	See Walk 24

This introductory stage can be cut to 3hr for an afternoon start. This first stage climbs easily to the Cabane des Becs de Bosson. For those inclined to avoid the steep piste climb under the lift, taking a ride to Bendolla saves 1hr 30min and 540m of uphill.

Above Bendolla the path climbs steadily on grassy slopes before entering the higher ski area where lifts and earthmoving have disrupted the high mountain environment. The stage finishes with a climb to the Col des Becs de Bosson and then to the cabane across wild, rocky terrain.

Views from the cabane are outstanding, especially the sunsets and sunrises. It's a welcoming place, although there is no running water. If time allows, the hard-looking alpine route on the rocky pinnacles of Becs de Bosson could be attempted, or an easier walk up the Pointe de la Tsevalire, with views into the protected Rèchy valley.

STAGE 2
Cabane des Becs de Bosson to Cabane de Moiry

Start	Cabane des Becs de Bosson (2982m)
Finish	Cabane de Moiry (2826m)
Distance	16.7km
Total ascent	850m
Total descent	1000m
Time	5hr 30min
Description	See Walk 25 and 26 (for the 2500m route)

This longish but straightforward route has an interesting final climb to the cabane. Views of the Lac de Moiry and Dent Blanche dominate the walk, then the Moiry icefall on the final climb.

After an initial drop to the Pas de Lona and the Lac de Lona, the route takes a track over the Basset de Lona (2791m) from where the nearby Ché (or Sex) de Mareinda can be climbed in 30min. The track continues downhill for another hour to the Alpage de Torrent (2480m, 2hr 30min).

Here there is a choice:
- Either follow the signed Tours des Cabanes routing down to just above the Moiry barrage and then alongside the lake to the parking at the end of the lake in 1hr 30min,

- or take the 2500m route that traverses high above the lake and descends at the end to the parking and Lac de Châteaupré, taking about 40min longer. For the walking and the outlook, this higher route is recommended, unless the weather is poor or deteriorating, in which case the quicker, lower route to the cabane is advised.

From the parking climb the 470m to the Cabane de Moiry. First climb the narrow moraine, then continue the climb on the rockier mountainside, all the time with closer views of the Moiry icefall, to arrive at the Cabane de Moiry (2826m), 5hr 30min from the start.

The cabane is one of the finest recent alpine constructions, beautifully laid out inside, and the outlook over the icefall and glaciers is exceptional.

STAGE 3

*Cabane de Moiry to
Cabane du Petit Mountet*

Start	Cabane de Moiry (2826m)
Finish	Cabane du Petit Mountet (2140m)
Distance	21.3km
Total ascent	1170m
Total descent	1860m
Time	7hr 30min
Description	See Walks 27 and 28

This is a long stage but there is the option to take the gondola for the last part of the descent to Zinal, where it would be possible to stay overnight and continue to Grand Mountet the following day.

Descend the route climbed the previous day and at the first turning at 2522m take the high traverse above the east side of Lac de Moiry. After 2hr 30min meet the ascending path from the barrage and climb steadily over the Col de Sorebois. Descend to the Vouarda (Espace Weisshorn) station and then the Sorebois station (both with gondola options) and descend directly to Zinal. You are on the signed Route 6 from the junction above the barrage onwards, and the path to Zinal negotiates the steep mountainside in well-made zigzags.

The Weisshorn and Zinalrothorn (and brass ibex sculpture) from Sorebois

From Zinal take the valley route and then the 1hr 30min climb to Petit Mountet, a welcoming, privately owned cabane perched above the moraine on the Glacier de Zinal.

For an adventure, a **blue alpine route** heads directly from the Sorebois station to Petit Mountet in about 3hr. This crosses steep and rocky landslips so be confident of your abilities and check first if in doubt.

It would be possible to overnight in Zinal, shortening the day and adding 2hr to the following stage, but this would miss out an overnight stay at Petit Mountet.

STAGE 4

Cabane du Petit Mountet to
Cabane du Grand Mountet

Start	Cabane du Petit Mountet (2140m)
Finish	Cabane du Grand Mountet (2886m)
Distance	8km
Total ascent	1100m
Total descent	350m
Time	4hr 15min
Description	See Walk 29

This is a shorter but still strenuous day. The path is well crafted, especially in view of the terrain it crosses, but the final boulder section, although fairly level and as well made as possible, is still tough going. The mountains around compensate in full for the effort expended.

Drop down by the track to the bridge over the Navisence (30min). Cross the bridge and turn right along the river. The climb starts after 10min, first up and

The Pointe de Zinal above the Glacier Durand from the
Cabane du Grand Mountet

along a moraine then steeply under cliffs before the more open mountainside of Besso. Pass a cross then a bridge over a gorge to reach a climb with cable support which is then followed by a lengthy-feeling 2km across boulder and scree to finally reach the cabane.

The **Cabane du Grand Mountet** looks out directly on the Ober Gabelhorn, with the Zinalrothorn and Dent Blanche and many lesser summits around.

STAGE 5

*Cabane du Grand Mountet to
Cabane Arpitettaz*

Start	Cabane du Grand Mountet (2886m)
Finish	Cabane Arpitettaz (2786m)
Distance	13km
Total ascent	990m
Total descent	1090m
Time	6hr
Description	See Walk 31

Starting with the long traverse along the flank of Besso and finishing at a small and wonderfully sited cabane, this is a day of exceptional mountain walking.

Reverse the climb, signed 2hr 30min to the Navisence bridge – more realistically 3hr. Climb past the river junctions and then above to reach the small and peaceful Lac d'Arpitettaz (4hr).

Onwards, the route has full views of the Weisshorn directly ahead and the Zinalrothorn and its glaciers to the right. The path climbs in steps. Cross a bridge before the final climb to the cabane.

Smaller than Grand Mountet, **Cabane Arpitettaz** in its position beneath the great peaks above is well worth the effort involved.

STAGE 6

Cabane Arpitettaz to
Cabane de Tracuit

Start	Cabane Arpitettaz (2786m)
Finish	Cabane de Tracuit (3259m)
Distance	10km
Total ascent	1170m
Total descent	700m
Time	5hr
Description	See Walks 30 and 32

The TCVA takes a lower route over the Roc de la Vache. For those with the right experience and mountain skills, a higher blue alpine route over the Col de Milon is available. This takes about 3hr to reach the cabane so could be combined with Stage 7, although this would miss out on a night at Tracuit, beautifully located on a col and looking out over the glaciers towards the Bishorn and Weisshorn, as well as the full panoply of peaks above Zinal.

Descend to the Lac d'Arpitettaz (1hr 30min) and climb the Roc de la Vache (2hr 30min). Drop 100m to meet the main Tracuit path. From here it's about 2hr to the cabane, climbing over a series of 'steps' before a final steep climb and then a short, rocky section protected by a chain to reach the cabane.

STAGE 7
Cabane de Tracuit to Zinal

Start	Cabane de Tracuit (3259m)
Finish	Zinal 1674m
Distance	9km
Total ascent	20m
Total descent	1610m
Time	3hr 15min
Description	See Walks 30 and 32

There is no getting away from this long descent to Zinal, although a diversion over the Roc de la Vache and Vichiesso is a more attractive option if time allows.

Descend the steep upper slopes and then the less steep grassy mountainside. Reach the 2478m junction in 1hr 30min and continue down to the 2254m junction in 2hr. Continue the long and rather undersigned descent to the parking at the end of the Zinal road and then turn right into Zinal.

The Roc de la Vache route adds 1hr to the descent. Turn left at the 2478m junction and climb the Roc, taking plenty of time to absorb the scenery. Descend to the Lac d'Arpitettaz and then the Navisence bridge. Turn right and follow the track past Le Vichiesso to the valley and so to Zinal.

Whichever route you take down, Zinal should provide the restoratives needed after over 85km and nearly 7000m of ascent and descent on mountainous ground in one week.

APPENDIX A
Contact information

Local tourist offices
Val d'Anniviers
www.valdanniviers.ch

Grimentz tourist office
Rue du Village 6
3961 Grimentz
+41 27 476 17 00

St Luc tourist office
Route Principale 18
3961 St-Luc
+41 27 476 17 10

Chandolin tourist office
Route des Plampras 9
3961 Chandolin
+41 27 476 17 15

Zinal tourist office
Route des Cinq 4000 14
3961 Zinal
+41 27 476 17 05

Vercorin tourist office
Route d'Anniviers 1
3967 Vercorin
+41 27 455 58 55
www.vercorin.ch

Val d'Hérens
www.valdherens.ch

Evolène region tourist office
Place Clos Lombard 6
1983 Evolène
+41 27 283 40 00
www.evolene-region.ch

Arolla tourist office and post office
Place de la Poste 1
1986 Arolla
+41 27 283 30 30
www.evolene-region.ch

Hérémence tourist office
Route Principale 19
1987 Hérémence
+41 27 281 15 33
www.heremence-tourisme.ch

St Martin tourist office
Rue de l'Evouette 7
1969 Saint-Martin
+41 27 281 24 74
www.stmt.ch

Tourist information
Switzerland Tourism (UK)
info.uk@myswitzerland.com
www.myswitzerland.com

Swiss National Tourist Office (USA)
+1 877 231 3523
info.usa@myswitzerland.com

Swiss Tourism (Australia)
www.myswitzerland.com/en-au

Swiss Alpine Club
www.sac-cas.ch/en

Swiss Hiking Trail Federation
www.schweizmobil.ch

Map suppliers
Stanfords
+44 207 836 1321
sales@stanfords.co.uk
www.stanfords.co.uk

The Map Shop
+44 1684 593146
0800 085 40 80 (UK only)
themapshop@btinternet.com
www.themapshop.co.uk

Swisstopo
www.swisstopo.admin.ch

USA
Omnimap.com

Apps

MeteoSwiss – Swiss weather forecasting

SBB Mobile – all Swiss public transport

SNCF Connect – French rail booking

SwitzerlandMobility – Swiss mapping

Swisstopo – Swisstopo mapping to buy
and download

PhoneMaps – open data mapping with
footpaths

Outdooractive – mapping and routes

Open data maps, with options to
purchase Swisstopo maps

Mountain huts and restaurants

Val d'Anniviers

Le Tsapé restaurant
+41 27 476 15 65

Cabane Bella-Tola
3961 St-Luc
+41 27 476 15 67
41 beds in rooms and small dormitories
cabane@funiluc.ch

Restaurant Tignousa
+41 27 476 15 55

Hotel Weisshorn
+41 27 475 11 06
57 beds, double and single rooms only
info@weisshorn.ch

Cabane des Becs de Bosson
3961 Grimentz
+41 78 /43 79 89
62 beds in 7 dormitories
info@cabanedesbecs.ch

Restaurant Bendolla
+41 27 476 20 15

Cabane Barrage de Moiry
+41 27 475 15 48 (groups only)

Cabane de Moiry CAS
3961 Grimentz
Same day booking by phone
+41 27 475 45 34
Otherwise, online booking only
www.cabane-moiry.ch

Relais de la Tzoucdana, Zinal
+41 27 475 12 19
info@tzoucdana

Cabane du Petit Mountet
3961 Zinal
+41 27 475 13 80
40 beds in small dormitories
petitmountet@bluewin.ch

Cabane du Grand Mountet
3961 Zinal
+41 27 475 14 31
100 dormitory beds
mountet@cas-diablerets.ch

Cabane Arpitettaz
3961 Zinal
+41 27 475 40 28
32 dormitory beds
cabane@arpitettaz.ch

Cabane de Tracuit
3961 Zinal
+41 27 475 15 00
120 beds in small dormitories
cabane@tracuit.ch

Val d'Hérens
Restaurant Le Petit Paradis (Ferpècle)
+41 27 283 10 44

Hotel de la Sage
+41 27 283 24 20
info@hoteldelasage.ch
lasage-boutiquehotel.com

Cabane de la Tza
+41 76 261 11 48
32 beds in 2 dormitories
cabtza@gmail.com

Cabane de Bertol CAS
+41 27 283 19 29
bertol@cas-neuchatel.ch

Cabane des Vignettes
+41 27 283 13 22
info@cabane-des-vignettes.ch

Cabane des Aiguilles Rouges
+41 27 283 16 49
70 dormitory beds
cabane@aiguillesrouges.c

Buvette du Lac d'Arbey
+41 78 908 00 89

Restaurant La Remointze (Chemeuille)
+41 27 283 20 35

Buvette and gîtes de l'alpage de Mandelon
+41 78 617 61 69

Hotel du Barrage (Dix)
+41 27 281 13 22

Cabane des Dix
+41 27 281 15 23
109 dormitory beds
info@cabanedesdix.ch

Cabane de Prafleuri
+41 27 281 17 80
59 dormitory beds
cabane.prafleuri@gmail.com

Cabane d'Essertze
+41 79 368 96 08
25 beds, in large dormitory and two 3-bed rooms

Camping

Val d'Anniviers
Camping d'Anniviers
Route des Landoux, Vissoie
+41 27 475 14 09
georgestheytaz@bluewin.ch

Camping du Pont d'Anniviers
Pont de Mission
3961 Ayer
+41 79 658 24 51
info@potentille.c

Camping Tzoucdana (adjacent to Relais de la Tzoucdana, Zinal)
+41 27 475 12 19
info@tzoucdana

Camping Llot Bosquet
Rte de Boccard, Grimentz
+41 27 476 17 00
grimentz@anniviers.ch

Val d'Hérens
Camping du Val d'Hérens, Vex
+41 27 207 19 85

Camping d'Evolène
+41 79 221 03 72
+41 27 283 11 44
info@camping-evolene.ch

Camping de Molignon, Les Haudères
+41 27 283 12 40
info@molignon.ch

Camping d'Arolla
Info@camping-arolla.ch
camping-arolla.ch

Camping du Val des Dix
+41 27 281 20 63
contact@val-des-dix.com

Lifts and funicular
Chandolin–Tsapé chairlift
Open 9:00–17:00 daily late June–mid
September
+41 27 465 1560

St Luc–Tignousa funicular
Open 8:00–17:00 (18:00 high season)
Every 30min
+41 27 465 1550

Grimentz–Bendolla gondola
Open 8:30–16:00, last descent 16:30

Grimentz–Espace Weisshorn gondola
Open 8:30–16:00, last descent 16:30

Zinal–Sorebois–Espace Weisshorn
gondola
Open 8:30–16:00, last descent 16:30

Evolène (Lannaz)–Chemeuille chairlift
Open 9:00–13:00, 14:15–17:00 daily
July–mid September
+41 27 283 1080

Outdoor gear shops

Arolla
Bournissen Sports
+41 27 283 14 54

Les Haudères
Chevrier Sports
+41 27 283 22 82

Quinodoz Sports
+41 27 283 10 10

Evolène
Sport Evasion
+41 27 283 22 11

La Forclaz
Crettaz Sports
+41 79 277 86 25

Zinal
Olympia Sports
+41 27 475 13 76

Zinal Sports
+41 27 475 60 58

Grimentz
Valsport
+41 27 475 27 76

Do Sports
+41 27 475 17 88

St Luc
Sport 4000-Christophe Salamin
+41 27 475 13 48

APPENDIX B

Glossary of useful French words

French	English
aiguille	needle-like peak
alpage	summer pasture
arête	ridge
batons	trekking poles
bouquetin	ibex
brouillard	fog
buvette	small café
cabane	mountain refuge
carte	map
cascade	waterfall
chambre d'hôte	bed and breakfast
chapelle	chapel
chemin	path
chèvre	goat
chute de pierre	rockfall
ciel	sky
col	pass, saddle
combe	shallow valley
commune	district (small)
corniche	overhanging mass of hardened snow at the end of a precipice
couloir	corridor (in mountain terms, a narrow passageway through rocks)
coup de soleil	sunstroke
crête	ridge
croix	cross
danger (dangereux)	danger (dangerous)
descendre	to go down
église	church
entrée interdite	no entry
est	east
étang	pond
falaise	cliff
ferme	farm
fleur	flower
gouffre	large hole, chasm
gouille	lake/tarn
grimper	to climb
haut/e	high
lac	lake
mairie	town hall
marcher (se promener)	to walk
météo	weather forecast
montagne	mountain
moraine	debris (rocks) carried down by a glacier
mouton	sheep

French	English
neige	snow
nord	north
nuage (nuageux)	cloud (cloudy)
oiseau	bird
orage	thunderstorm
ouest	west
pas	pass
pic	peak or summit
piste	track (usually meaning a man-made path for skiers)
pluie	rain
pointe	point or peak
pont	bridge
pré/praz	meadow
propriété privée	private property

French	English
randonnée	long walk
ravin	ravine, gully
rivière	river
rocher	rock
route	road
sac à dos	rucksack
sentier	marked path
sommet	summit
source	spring (water)
sud	south
télécabine	cable car
télésiège	chairlift
temps	weather
vache	cow
vallée	valley
versant	side (of a mountain)

NOTES

NOTES

DOWNLOAD THE ROUTES
IN GPX FORMAT

All the routes in this guide are available for download from:

www.cicerone.co.uk/1096/GPX

as standard format GPX files. You should be able to load them into most online GPX systems and mobile devices, whether GPS or smartphone. You may need to convert the file into your preferred format using a conversion programme such as gpsvisualizer.com or one of the many other such websites and programmes.

When you follow this link, you will be asked for your email address and where you purchased the guidebook, and have the option to subscribe to the Cicerone e-newsletter.

www.cicerone.co.uk

CICERONE

Trust Cicerone to guide your next adventure,
wherever it may be around the world...

Discover guides for hiking, mountain walking, backpacking,
trekking, trail running, cycling and mountain biking, ski touring,
climbing and scrambling in Britain, Europe and worldwide.

Connect with Cicerone online and find inspiration.

- buy books and ebooks
- articles, advice and trip reports
- GPX files and updates
- regular newsletter

cicerone.co.uk